WALKING IN TOTAL
God-Confidence

Bethany House Books
by Donna Partow

Becoming a Vessel God Can Use
Families That Play Together Stay Together
(with Cameron Partow)
How to Work With the One You Love (with Cameron Partow)
No More Lone Ranger Moms
Walking in Total God-Confidence

WALKING IN TOTAL

God-Confidence

DONNA PARTOW

BETHANY HOUSE PUBLISHERS
MINNEAPOLIS, MINNESOTA 55438

Library of Congress Cataloging-in-Publication Data

Partow, Donna.
   Walking in total God-confidence / by Donna Partow .
      p.   cm.
   ISBN 0–7642–2185–X (pbk.)
   1. Trust in God—Christianity. 2. Trust in God—Christianity Meditations.
3. Partow, Donna. 4. Self-confidence—Religious aspects—Christianity.
5. Suffering—Religious aspects—Christianity. I. Title.
BV4637.P37   1999
248.8'43—dc21   99–6379
                                                                      CIP

To Nichole Alexandra,
who always walks in Total God-Confidence.

"The Lord turned to him and said,
'Go in the strength you have. . . .
Am I not sending you?' "

Judges 6:14 NIV

DONNA PARTOW is a Christian communicator with a compelling testimony of God's transforming power. From her childhood as "the kid no one was allowed to play with" to her days as a drug dealer and her marriage to a strict Middle Eastern husband, she shares her life journey with disarming honesty and humor.

Donna's uncommon transparency and passion for Christ have been used by God at women's conferences and retreats around the country. She has been a popular guest on more than one hundred radio and TV programs, including *Focus on the Family*.

She is the bestselling author of numerous books including *Becoming a Vessel God Can Use*.

If your church sponsors an annual women's retreat, perhaps they would be interested in learning more about Donna's special weekend program on "Walking in Total God-Confidence." For more information, contact:

Donna Partow
P.O. Box 842
Payson, AZ 85541
(520) 472–7368
e-mail: donnapartow@cybertrails.com

Special Thanks

My heavenly Father, who wasn't kidding when he said, "The burden will be light this time." Wow, this was almost too easy!

Steve Laube, my editor, who now has a full-day's supply of fresh stories to tell. Now, where did I put that toothbrush?

Kevin Johnson and the team at Bethany House, who continue to believe I have a message worth printing.

Betty Fitch and Helen Storm for lending their spiritual and editorial insight. Most of all, thanks for being my prayer warriors.

How to Get the Most
Out of This Study

Leah, my eight-year-old daughter, loves to read. During the last school year, she read 100 books. Among her favorites was a child's version of John Bunyan's classic *Pilgrim's Progress* entitled *Dangerous Journey*. Many of you have probably read *Pilgrim's Progress*, which is an allegory of the Christian life.[1]

In a very real sense, this ten-week journey to walking in Total God-Confidence is a dangerous journey. Just like Pilgrim, we'll have to slog through the mud and the mire, through desert wastelands, up over rugged mountains, and across raging rivers. To make matters worse, we even have an enemy prowling around like a roaring lion looking for someone to devour.

We are not gonna make it in high heels! This is not a cruise vacation to Total God-Confidence! It's a journey. And sometimes the journey is going to be tough. It's going to take you through some hard, hard places. I guarantee it. However, the rewards will far outweigh the sacrifices.

The enemy of your soul does *not* want you to grab hold of the truths contained on these pages. He doesn't want you to be daily in God's Word. He doesn't want you to be part of a weekly accountability group. So don't be surprised when everything goes wrong the night before or the morning of your weekly gathering. The kids will get the flu, the car will break down, you'll suddenly have an unbearable headache. Or you won't feel an immediate connection with the women in your class, you won't like the leader's style, or maybe you'll

[1]Oliver Hunkin, *Dangerous Journey: The Story of Pilgrim's Progress* (illus.) (Grand Rapids, Mich.: Eerdmans, 1985). Whether or not you've read the complete version, I would strongly encourage you to obtain *Dangerous Journey*. Read and enjoy it alone or with children of all ages.

even have a personality conflict with another woman in the group.

Mentally prepare yourself now. Make the commitment. *I will finish this journey I've started, no matter what it takes.*

Now for some practical matters. First, although you can certainly take this journey alone, I would encourage you to take it with friends. Ideally, this study should be completed as part of a weekly women's Bible study. However, you can gather informally with a small group of women or just one friend. The idea is to have someone holding you accountable to finish what you've started.

Second, if possible, quickly read through the entire book to get an overview. Then go back and work through the study one day at a time, carefully answering the questions and studying the review material.

Third, take the Review Test every week. Allow the principles to become part of your life, so that when you have finished the study you'll take them with you.

Fourth, memorize the weekly verses. It's easy to do, if you'll simply cut out the verse cards included in the back of the book. Carry them with you wherever you go, and when you have a spare minute, meditate on them. If you like, you can have the cards laminated for longer durability . . . and in case you spill your coffee on them! When the study is through, you'll have memorized ten verses. More importantly, you'll have acquired the habit of Scripture memory and meditation.

I pray that today will be more than the first day of a devotional book. I pray that it will be the first day of your lifelong journey toward walking in Total God-Confidence.

Contents

WEEK FOUR: FREE FROM THE CHAINS THAT BIND

WEEK FIVE: INCREASINGLY CONFORMED
TO HIS CHARACTER

WEEK SIX: DAILY IN HIS WORD

WEEK SEVEN: ENERGIZED BY FAITH

Contents

WEEK ONE:
Called
According to His Purpose

This Week's Verse:

O Lord, we love to do your will! Our hearts' desire
is to glorify your name.

Isaiah 26:8

Day One

Self-Confidence Versus God-Confidence

O Israel, if you will truly return to me and absolutely discard your idols, and if you will swear by me alone, the living God, and begin to live good, honest, clean lives, then you will be a testimony to the nations of the world and they will come to me and glorify my name.   Jeremiah 4:1–2

I'm always amused when people say I come across as a very self-confident person. Having been my own constant companion lo these many years, I can assure you that nothing could be further from the truth.

I know myself too well to have any confidence in my own ability or my own goodness. In fact, as the years go by, I'm increasingly confident of only one thing: left to my own devices and given the opportunity to blow it, I'll blow it every time.

Have you ever met someone possessed of an uncanny ability to make the worst of a good situation? The kind of person who invents new ways of sabotaging herself? That's me. You know the slogan "If it ain't broke, don't fix it"? Well, my motto is "If it ain't broke, break it and watch what happens. Someday I'm going to be a "Giant of the Christian Faith" and I'll stop doing incredibly dumb stuff all the time. Meanwhile, I'm stuck with the real me. As a result, I have zero self-confidence.

When I was just getting started as a professional speaker, I attended a secular training conference where the leader advised, "Fake it till you make it. Dress to the nines and act like you know what you're doing. The audience will never know the difference." Well, that sounded like great advice to me. I knew I hadn't "made it" but I figured I could "fake it." So, when I finally got my first speaking engagement, I was nervous . . . but at least I had a strategy.

Even though my husband was unemployed and we were flat broke, I just had to have a new outfit. So, out came the credit card and off I went to the local mall. (I say this to my shame.) Well, I found this fabulous purple outfit with gold buttons—very confident-looking. *Perfect*, I thought, *they won't notice that I'm trembling down to my ankles. All they'll notice is this great suit.*

Everything seemed to go fine at the event and my confidence level started climbing out of the basement. *Hey, maybe God really has called me to do this!* About a week later, I got a letter in the mail postmarked from the city I had just spoken in. *Fan mail*, I thought. *This is too cool.* I opened it expectantly. Guess what? The woman commented on what a nice suit I wore. That was the good part. Then she added, "I couldn't really concentrate on what you were saying because your hair was such a mess. Maybe you should cut it shorter."

How would you react to a letter like that?

I'll tell you what I did: I put that letter down and immediately walked over to my neighbor's house (she's a former hairstylist) and told her to "cut it all off." Boy, did she cut it all off! Then I went to the grocery store and bought a bag of Oreos and a gallon of milk. After I polished that off, I hid under the covers for a month, vowing never to speak in public again.

For the record, I look awful in short hair.

When I finally crawled out from under the covers and snapped out of my Oreo-induced depression, God began to show me that there was a better way. That I didn't have to go through life faking it and trying desperately to make it.

He began to teach me that there's another kind of confidence . . . a much better confidence! It's God-Confidence, and it's something completely different. God-Confidence is absolute assurance that God can do whatever he wants through whomever he chooses. It's confidence that God can—and often does—choose to work through the last person on earth that human beings would choose.

God-Confidence trusts completely that God has a purpose for your life and that he is more than capable of seeing it fulfilled. It's confidence that he can even use a woman who's having a bad hair day. (I never have bad hair days; I have a bad hair LIFE.)

You see, your level of self-confidence is based on your level of trust in your own ability. To determine your level, you (consciously or subconsciously) take a little inventory of your resources, looking at factors like:

- who your parents were
- what kind of family life you had
- what schools you went to
- which side of the tracks you grew up on
- how long you've been a Christian
- how mature you consider yourself as a Christian
- how well you perform certain Christian rituals such as praying, reading your Bible, attending Sunday school, etc.
- the condition of your marriage and family life
- your status in the church and community
- how others treat you
- how you judge your own personal appearance
- your past successes and failures
- thousands of other personal and cultural criteria.

Then, based on that analysis, you come to some conclusions about what you can and cannot do, about what can and cannot be accomplished through your life.

Self-confidence looks inward; God-Confidence looks upward. Which one is your life based upon?

I'll be honest. On the days when I operate according to self-confidence, I can barely get out of bed. The awareness of my weaknesses and failures overwhelms me. But on the days when I walk in Total God-Confidence, look out, world! Right now I'm averaging about three days out of seven in God-Confidence; the other four days I fail to look upward, and my life shows it.

My goal in writing this book is to challenge myself, even as I challenge you, to walk *every day* in Total God-Confidence. Confidence is defined by *Webster's Dictionary*[1] as "faith, trust, and assurance." That's what we need. Faith. Trust. And assurance. It also defines it as "a reliance on another's discretion." Wow. That's the heart of the matter, isn't it? If we can come to the place where we *rely on God's discretion* rather than our own—when we can say from our hearts,

---

[1]*Webster's Dictionary* (Springfield, Mass.: G. & C. Merriam Co., 1978).

"Lord, you know best. You decide"—we'll truly be walking in Total God-Confidence.

That's the purpose of this ten-week journey, and I'm excited that we're taking it together.

I consider it an incredible privilege to be a writer and a great honor that you're reading my book. I know how hectic and downright frustrating life can be. I know what it's like to be searching for solutions. I know what it is to pick up a book and cry out with a desperate prayer to heaven, "Lord, use this to change me! I need a breakthrough in my life!"

I know what it's like to get a few pages into a book and think, "What planet is this woman living on? Not only is she perfect, her house is perfect, her church is perfect, her marriage is perfect, her kids and grandkids are perfect, her dog is perfect, even her neighbors are perfect. Is she for real?" And you hope like crazy that the answer is NO, otherwise, you're worse off than you thought you were when you picked up the book in the first place.

I think you'll find that I'm living on the same crazy, mixed-up planet you're living on, that I encounter the same mix of fruits and nuts you do. I don't live in a perfect world. I live in a world where people (including me) do incredibly stupid things. My kids aren't perfect. My marriage isn't perfect. And my spices aren't in alphabetical order.

But I have found the perfect solution to all this madness: placing my confidence in the only One who IS perfect.

My guess is that you picked up this book because you wanted something different, something more, from your Christian life. I can't give you any guarantees, but I'll tell you this much: the principles I'm about to share with you have truly changed my life. I'm finding, deep within, a quiet confidence in God that I never thought I could experience. And that confidence isn't based on a magic formula. It's not "fake it till you make it." It's based on who God is. I'm convinced that the more we know of God, the more confidence we will have. That's why, on this ten-week journey, we won't be seeking confidence; we'll be seeking God.

It's my prayer that this book will enable you to grow in your knowledge *of God*, which must inevitably lead to increased confidence *in God*.

Take Time to Reflect

1. Rate your self-confidence level.

2. Rate your God-Confidence level.

3. Do you walk according to self-confidence or God-Confidence? How can you tell?

4. What do you hope to gain from this study? List some specific goals.

5. Look up Proverbs 3:13 and note God's word of encouragement for you.

6. Write out a prayer to God, expressing your desire to grow in your knowledge of him and in your ability to walk in Total God-Confidence.

7. What key lesson did you glean from today's study?

8. Turn to the back of the book and remove your Bible verse card for this week.

Confidence Boosters:

- God-Confidence is absolute assurance that God can do whatever he wants through whomever he chooses.
- Increased knowledge *of God* inevitably leads to increased confidence *in God*.
- On this journey, we won't be seeking confidence; we'll be seeking God.

Day Two

Put On the Boots

I want to tell you about a very special pair of boots that have found a permanent place in my heart. They are size 9, eight-inch-high construction boots and they belong to my now-sixteen-year-old daughter Nikki. But before I can tell you about the boots, I have to back up and tell you how Nikki came into my life.

In 1994, after four years of waiting, I became pregnant with my second child. Everything went well with the pregnancy until the fourth month, when I miscarried. It was a devastating experience, but with the help of God and close friends, I got through the initial loss. I can remember thinking, "Okay, the only thing left to survive is the due date, August 28. If I can get through that, I'll be okay." I just knew that, somehow, God had a purpose in my loss, and I was on the watch for it.

On August 26 I received a call on the church prayer chain about a twelve-year-old girl who was in desperate need of a home because both of her parents had been taken off to prison. The minute I heard the request, my heart leapt within me. Suddenly everything made sense. This was the very week our baby had been due. It was as if God had taken our baby to heaven early so there would be room in our home and room in our hearts for this young girl.

The best part was, I could send out the birth announcements after all: *It's a girl. 5'4", 120 lbs.*

Within two days Nikki came to live with us. Gradually her story began to unfold. We discovered that she had lived in some fifty different places, including in cars. She had been knocked around from place to place, being rejected over and over. Some families kept her for a few days, some for a few weeks. Believe it or not, one family kept her for *half an hour*.

As you can imagine, Nikki had zero self-confidence.

But God began to do a miraculous work in her life. He began convincing her that he had great plans for her future. About a year later she felt God was calling her to be a missionary to Africa. She heard about an organization called Teen Missions, which offers short-term mission assignments to teenagers. She put in her application, got accepted, and everything was in motion. Talk about walking in Total God-Confidence. She was so excited, I thought she would burst. She just *knew* this was part of God's purpose.

Nikki was told that the very first thing she needed to do to prepare for this great mission assignment was to buy a pair of 8-inch-high construction boots, put them on right away, and wear them every day to break them in.

Well, she sent away for the boots. Then she sent out her missionary support letter to raise the $5,000 it was going to cost to get her there. And, uh, not much happened.

Boy, did that shoot her confidence. Suddenly she wanted ALL the answers up front. "Okay, God. Where's the money gonna come from? When is it gonna arrive? What color check is it gonna be printed on? How's it all gonna work out?"

She literally refused to put on those boots! In essence, her attitude was, "God, I'm not taking one more step—I'm not even going to put on my boots until you give me all the answers up front." I'm telling you, sisters, those boots sat around our house for three months with the tags still on them.

Now you're probably sitting there thinking, "O she of little faith." But let me ask you something: Have you put your boots on? Is there something God has called you to do, but since he hasn't given you ALL the answers up front, you're not willing to take a step of faith? Not even willing to put on the boots?

A. W. Tozer, in his book *The Knowledge of the Holy*, says this:

> Most of us go through life praying a little, planning a little, jockeying for position, hoping but never being quite certain of anything, and always secretly afraid that we will miss the way. This is a tragic waste of truth and never gives rest to the heart. There is a better way. It is to repudiate our own wisdom and take instead the infinite wisdom of God.[1]

---

[1] A. W. Tozer, *The Knowledge of the Holy* (HarperSan Francisco [reprint], 1978).

Now listen carefully to this part:

> *Our insistence upon seeing ahead is natural enough, but it is a real hindrance to our spiritual progress* [emphasis added]. God has charged himself with full responsibility for our eternal happiness. And he stands ready to take over the management of our lives the moment we turn in faith to him.

He stands ready, sisters. But first we have to come to the place where we consider—and this is a big thought—that maybe, just maybe, God can do a better job of managing our lives than we have done. Just a thought.

When we insist on seeing ahead, knowing the answers up front, we can't walk in Total God-Confidence. In fact, we stop dead in our tracks. *We refuse to even put on the boots.* Some of us won't even take off the tags.

If you're ready to make real spiritual progress, don't insist on knowing the answers up front. Just put on your boots and walk forward in Total God-Confidence, knowing that you have been called according to his purpose.

Take Time to Reflect

1. Is there something God has called you to do, but since he hasn't given you all the answers up front, you're not willing to take a step of faith?

2. Can you think of a specific step you can take that will be for you, in essence, "putting on the boots"?

3. Look up Proverbs 3:5 and note God's word of encouragement for you today.

4. Write out a prayer to God, asking him for courage to "put on the boots."

5. What key lesson did you glean from today's study?

Confidence Boosters:

- Our insistence upon seeing ahead is natural enough, but it's a real hindrance to our spiritual progress.
- Don't wait until you have all the answers up front. Be willing to "put on the boots" and take a step of faith.

Day Three

What Has Shaken Your Confidence?

H as your confidence been shaken? Was there a time when you believed God had great things for you, but then something happened and you lost hope?

Today I want to tell you about the event that first shook my confidence in the world. It was when my oldest brother returned from Vietnam a heroin addict. For reasons I've struggled my whole life to understand, somehow there was fertile soil in our family. Eventually four of my seven siblings developed an addiction to the drug. Suddenly we were the "bad news" family. The drug addict family. And I was the kid in the neighborhood that no one was supposed to play with.

The kids in my class used to torment me relentlessly. They would draw pictures of my family with needles in our arms and write "Drug Addict Family" across the top. I'll never forget one day in particular when the teacher stepped out of the room. All the kids in my class formed a circle around me and sang, "DRUG ADDICT FAMILY, DRUG ADDICT FAMILY, DRUG ADDICT FAMILY" until I couldn't stand it anymore and ran home crying.

Now for the real irony. After seeing the human carnage, the wreckage drugs caused, after seeing them tear my family apart and rob me of my childhood, guess what I became? I'll tell you, when the Hound of Heaven tracked me down and dragged me kicking and screaming into the kingdom of God, I was not only a drug addict, I was a drug dealer. I was the kind of scum who would give your kid free drugs just to get him hooked and land a long-term customer.

But I praise God that he did not leave me in that place. In July 1980 I received a phone call from an old high school friend, Bruce Bacon. He said there was a really neat camp in northern Pennsylvania. The setting was breathtaking and the people were fabulous.

He said it started the following day, and he concluded the conversation by saying, "I'm paying your way, so you can't say no. I'm picking you up tomorrow at 5:00 A.M."

I hung up the phone and figured, "Hey, what have I got to lose? It's a free vacation." I quickly packed my bags, including my string bikini and a couple of joints (that's marijuana cigarettes, for the uninitiated). Boy, was I in for a big surprise! Of course, I wasn't nearly as surprised as the Christian camp directors were when I showed up!

For the first couple of days I argued with them and generally made their lives miserable. Then one day I was sitting on the bank of the Delaware River when it suddenly became real to me: even if I were the only person on the planet, Jesus Christ would have gone to the Cross to pay the price for my sins. I was filled with an inexpressible joy. From that moment on, I've never had a single craving for drugs. That from a person who could not make it until 10:00 in the morning without getting high. What a miracle-working God we have!

The next night, there was a beautiful moon in the sky. As I walked along the river, gazing at the wonder of God's creation, I heard him speak to me in a way that was so clear, it was like he was walking next to me. He said, "I'm going to take you to retreat centers just like this one, all over the country. And I'm going to use you in a mighty way to make a difference in this world."

Let me tell you, I was excited! I was sending away for the boots. After all, I knew John 3:16. I figured it would take me a couple of months to get a handle on the Bible; a few more months to get my name out; and I'd be speaking at retreat centers before you could say hermeneutics! To tell you the truth, by the end of the week, I was ready to say to the guy teaching the camp, "You can sit down. I'll take it from here."

I can assure you, it didn't quite work out that way. I'll tell you the rest of my story tomorrow. For now, I want you to recall where you were when the Hound of Heaven tracked you down, and spend a few moments thanking him for his mercy to you. We all have a story to tell.

Take Time to Reflect

1. Can you recall an event in your life that shook your confidence?

2. Write out your personal testimony of coming to faith in Christ. Be prepared to share it with your classmates if you are doing this study in a group.

3. Look up Psalm 75:1 and note God's word of encouragement for you today.

4. What key lesson did you glean from today's study?

Confidence Boosters:

- Sometimes life can shake our confidence.
- We all have a story to tell of God's mercy and faithfulness.

Day Four

Staying Confident When Nothing Makes Sense

Two months after my moonlight encounter with God, I went off to college. During the first week I met a young Iranian man who was to change my life forever. I had grown up in a home that was completely out of control. Believe me, when you have four heroin addicts, you have a world that's out of control. So when I met this young man, I thought, *Now here is someone who has got things under control. Here's someone who can help me get my life under control.*

Did he get my life under control?

Oh my!

This was in the midst of the Iranian Hostage Crisis. Little did I know I was about to endure an Iranian hostage crisis of my own. You see, I married that young Iranian man. For the next ten years I was not allowed to leave my house unsupervised. Ten years. I was not allowed to drive. I was not allowed to go to a grocery store, not even allowed to walk to the corner convenience store to pick up a bottle of milk. I don't want to get bogged down in gory details here. Let me just put it this way: my husband exerted total control over my life.

One Saturday morning stands out in my mind. I woke up to an absolutely glorious day—a rarity in New Jersey—and I wanted so much to go for a walk around the block. Of course, such activities were completely forbidden, but I thought maybe, just maybe, this once. . . . I remember cautiously asking my husband. And the answer was no. So I asked, "Can I at least sit on the front steps?" The answer was no.

At that moment I couldn't help wondering, *What on earth happened to my life? What happened to my dreams? What happened to that glorious vision of a retreat ministry?*

I wish I could say that all during those years I continued to walk forward in Total God-Confidence. But how can I lie on the pages of a Christian book? I can remember during those years tormenting myself: *God, didn't you say what I thought you said? I mean, the one time I actually heard a voice from heaven and I got the message wrong? How am I going to travel around the country when I can't even walk around the block? How is all this gonna work out, Lord? I want the answers up front!*

In short, I refused to put on my boots. I refused to prepare. I realize now that those years—the "Dark Years"—were, in a strange way, a gift. They were my season of preparation. I should have walked forward in Total God-Confidence, knowing that God would bring about his perfect plan for my life. But I looked at my circumstances rather than looking at God. As a result, I completely lost confidence. I completely lost hope.

I did have one thing going for me, though: I firmly believed that God would deliver me—that he had a higher purpose for my life. I believed that somehow, some way, he would make sense out of the senseless mess I'd made of my life. I knew I couldn't possibly deliver myself. So I waited. And I prayed.

You'll find out later in the book how this story ends. I know, I know, it's a dirty trick! But I want you to finish reading this book.

For now, let me just say this: I never dreamed seventeen years would transpire from the time God "called me according to his purpose" until the time the vision would be fulfilled. But that's how long it took. I am living proof that God will do what he has promised. But not necessarily in the way we think he should and definitely not in our timing. That's because God's ways are not our ways and his timing is measured with instruments we know nothing about.

Nevertheless, we have been called according to his purpose and the one who began a good work in us *will* bring it to completion. It may not look that way right now, but we've got his Word on it.

Will you continue to walk in Total God-Confidence, even when nothing makes sense?

Take Time to Reflect

1. Is there something in your life right now that just doesn't make sense?

2. Look up Jeremiah 29:11 and note the promise God offers you.

3. Write a prayer of commitment to God that you will continue to walk in Total God-Confidence anyway!

4. What key lesson did you glean from today's study?

Confidence Boosters:

- God-Confidence continues to walk forward even when nothing makes sense.
- God's deliverance may not come the way we think it should, but it will come.
- God will do what he has promised, but not in our timing.

Day Five

Am I Not Sending You?

S ince I've decided to leave you hanging on my marriage story, I figured it was heartless not to finish Nikki's story.

Sometimes putting on the boots means trying the unconventional. First, Nikki tried to raise money in the usual way: by sending out prayer letters. We had it all figured out: fifty families in the church (hey, that wasn't asking much, the church had a thousand people) would each commit to $25 for four months. Piece of cake.

It didn't work that way.

Then we heard that other kids' youth groups had volunteered to do fund-raisers. *Aha!* we thought. *Get those kids moving for a good cause. Maybe some of them will catch the spirit and take a mission trip themselves.* But when Nikki approached one of the youth group leaders, the response was:

"You're awfully young. I think if you want to go on a mission trip you should get a job and save up for a few years. Why do you want to go on a mission trip anyway?"

Hmmm. Let's see. Plan C.

Nikki was ready to pitch the boots in the trash when I came up with a novel idea: Let's check out the Bible and see if we can find any ideas in there. (What a mom, eh?) Hey, how about the apostle Paul? He worked as a tentmaker to pay his own way. Maybe Nikki could be a tentmaker, too.

The whole family started brainstorming for tentmaking ideas. Then Nikki came up with a winner. She would design and "manufacture" cloth bookmarks to sell at my conferences. As it happened, I had a huge women's conference (well, the women weren't huge, but there was a huge number of them) called Women of Virtue scheduled for the following week. Nikki set to work.

She designed a cloth bookmark that involved a several-step process: ironing the cloth; putting some "heat and bond" between two pieces and ironing it again; cutting the cloth into bookmarks; hole-punching each bookmark; cutting ribbon; threading it through the bookmark and tying it in a bow. I share the entire process with you because it was a *huge* undertaking. (Yeah, huge is today's official word.)

She worked day and night. I vividly remember the night before the big event. Nikki traveled with me to Tucson, Arizona. We had dinner in the hotel, then went back to the room. She sat there for hours cutting fabric, until there was a purple indentation in her hand from the pressure. Tears were streaming down her face. "Why don't you stop now?" I urged. "No," she declared, "I'm going to do this!" I knew at that instant she had truly "put on the boots."

The next day, after sharing my "Walking in Total God-Confidence" message for the very first time, I called Nikki up to the stage with the words, "I have something I want to give you!" I gave her a giant hug, handed her the boots, and shared the story of Gideon:

> *The angel of the Lord came and sat down under the oak in Ophrah that belonged to Joash the Abiezrite, where his son Gideon was threshing wheat in a winepress to keep it from the Midianites. When the angel of the Lord appeared to Gideon, he said, "The Lord is with you, mighty warrior."*
>
> *"But sir," Gideon replied, "if the Lord is with us, why has all this happened to us? Where are all his wonders that our fathers told us about when they said, 'Did not the Lord bring us up out of Egypt?' But now the Lord has abandoned us and put us in the hand of Midian."*
>
> *The Lord turned to him and said, "Go in the strength you have and save Israel out of Midian's hand. Am I not sending you?"*
>
> *"But Lord," Gideon asked, "how can I save Israel? My clan is the weakest in Manasseh, and I am the least in my family."*
>
> *The Lord answered, "I will be with you"* (Judges 6:11–16 NIV).

Gideon wasn't exactly oozing self-confidence, was he? In essence he was saying, "God, I can't do what you're asking me to do! I'm just a kid. Besides, I'm from a lousy family." What's worse, he didn't even have God-Confidence! His attitude was "Yeah, some God you are.

You want me to save the people, and you haven't even been able to do it."

Nevertheless, he was called according to God's purpose. Gideon didn't need to know all the answers up front. He only needed to know three things. First, he needed to "go in the strength he had." Even though he didn't think he had much strength to go on, God said, "Go anyway." Second, he was to go because it's not about going, it's about the one who's sending. The Lord said, "Am I not sending you?" If God is sending us, we can walk in Total God-Confidence! Why? Because of the final promise: "I will be with you."

I told Nikki I believed with all my heart that God was sending her. Then I reminded her of a speaking event we had done together—an event I had orchestrated—that went very badly. When we sat in the car afterward, Nikki turned to me and said, "God didn't send us here, did he?"

"No," I whispered in shame. From that day on, we had resolved never to go anywhere unless God was sending us.

Now I reminded her of that vow. "Nikki, if God isn't sending you to Africa, believe me, you don't want to go. But if he is sending you, nothing on earth can stop you from going."

Nikki later told me that when she walked on stage, God spoke to her heart and told her, "Someday you will be the one with the microphone. You will be the one sharing your testimony about me." She knew at that moment that she wanted to be a Christian author and speaker.

That day she raised $742—most of it in $1 donations. Some ladies donated $5, $10, or $20—shoving the money into her boots, which were set up on my book table. The women were almost as excited as Nikki. Over the next several months, Nikki made almost four thousand bookmarks and raised $5,000 at Women of Virtue conferences around the country. (Thanks for your encouragement. We WOV you, ladies!)

The story gets even better: I hit upon the idea of encouraging the women to *pray for Nikki every time they looked at the bookmark.* Can you imagine? Rather than fifty families in our own church supporting her, suddenly she had *thousands* of women all over the country praying for her. She even received letters of support from Sunday school classes around the country that had taken up her cause.

Even now, years later, I still have women come up to me at conferences and ask, "How was Nikki's mission trip?" Then they add, "You know, I still pray for her whenever I look at that bookmark."

God's plan was so much better than ours, wasn't it? We didn't get all the answers up front, but wow, what an incredible answer we got!

However, none of it could have happened until Nikki took the step of faith and put on the boots.

When we returned from the conference, we filled our house with giant posters that posed the question: *Who's Sending You?*

Nikki did indeed go to Africa, where she spent three life-changing months as a missionary. I remember two letters in particular. In one she wrote, "I've fallen in love, but not with a man, with a country." And in another she wrote, "I know you probably have my school year planned already (we homeschool), but if it's all right with you, I'd like to spend the whole first semester just studying God's Word."

I wrote back, "Well, maybe just this once!" And do you know, she stuck to her purpose. Her entire curriculum consisted of reading the Bible, Bible commentaries, devotional guides, and great Christian thinkers like C. S. Lewis. By the end of the semester, she could easily beat the kids who'd been raised in Christian homes at Bible trivia games. More importantly, she had made tremendous strides in her spiritual growth.

What is God calling you to do? Are you living like you believe you've been *called according to his purpose*? If we know who's sending us, then we know all there is to know. The rest is just details. That's the kind of faith that energizes us! Let me ask you this: Are you afraid to step out in faith to do what God is asking you to do? If so, just remember who's sending you and walk forward with Total God-Confidence.

Take Time to Reflect

1. Where is God sending you?

2. Write out a prayer, expressing your desire to "go in the strength you have."

3. What key lesson did you glean from today's study?

4. Write out This Week's Verse from memory.

Confidence Boosters:

- The most important question you can ask is: "Who is sending me?"
- If God is not sending you, you don't want to go.
- If God is sending you, nothing on earth can stop you from going.

Weekly Review:

See if you can fill in the ten characteristics of walking in Total God-Confidence. Don't worry, this exercise will get easier as the weeks progress. For now, look in the back of the book if you need help.

C_____ according to his purpose

O_____ to his plan

N_____ by his love

F_____ from the chains that bind

I_____ conformed to his character

D_____ in his Word

E_____ by faith

N_____ shaken by the jerks

C_____ that he is able and faithful

E_____ to take the leap of faith

WEEK TWO:

Open
to His Plan

This Week's Verse:

Therefore, since we are surrounded by such a great cloud of
witnesses, let us throw off everything that hinders and the
sin that so easily entangles, and let us run with perseverance
the race marked out for us. Let us fix our eyes on Jesus, the
author and perfecter of our faith.

Hebrews 12:1–2

Day One

Run Your Own Race

Hebrews 12:1–2 says, "Therefore, since we are surrounded by such a great cloud of witnesses, let us throw off everything that hinders and the sin that so easily entangles, and let us run with perseverance the race marked out for us. Let us fix our eyes on Jesus, the author and perfecter of our faith."

I have to make a confession here. I don't know about the rest of you, but too often I am a woman on the run. Not really sure where I'm going or why I'm in such a hurry to get there, but I'm a-runnin' nevertheless. In fact, I've lived most of my life guided by the motto of the French Foreign Legion: "When in doubt . . . GALLOP!"

Sound familiar?

When I first became a Christian, I wanted so much to do great things for God. And I was absolutely sincere. Since my husband wasn't about to let me travel around the country speaking at women's retreats—the work God had called me to do—I decided to come up with other stuff I could do for God instead. So I poured myself into every ministry opportunity that came along.[1] My Sunday school teaching experience ranged from kindergarten all the way up to junior and senior high school. I taught Vacation Bible School to two- and three-year-olds. I didn't know why the lady who recruited me was so pleased when I agreed to do it. I found out. My husband and I hosted small group Bible studies in our home for nearly a decade. People just thought we were a very "tight" couple; most had no idea just how "tight" we really were!

When the Billy Graham Crusade came to the city of Philadelphia, we were the very first people signed up to help out. I was on

---

[1]Please understand, I could leave my house, but not unsupervised. My local church ministries were always under the watchful eye of my husband.

the fellowship committee. I was on the casserole committee—it didn't matter that I couldn't cook. If there was a committee, I was on it. I was going to do great things for God.

One of my favorite projects was my family. I've got a mom, dad, and seven older brothers and sisters who brought with them husbands, wives, nieces, nephews. Just a sea of humanity. And I was determined to win them all for Christ. I was constantly inviting them to church, to the Crusade, to Christian concerts, anywhere I thought God might be at work. I was lending them books, giving them tapes, all the time plotting and planning for their salvation. And finally, I'm happy to report, God poured forth his mercy upon my family. *He moved me out of state.*

As you can see, I certainly wasn't lacking in zeal. One thing I do have is an abundance of energy and a willing spirit. But no matter how hard I tried, it rarely seemed that God was really using me in people's lives. Oh, sure, occasionally it looked like something I'd said or done had made a difference, but in proportion to the amount of energy I was pouring forth, the returns were dismal.

I felt frustrated and exhausted. I had scattered my energies in a thousand different directions but saw little fruit. To tell you the truth, the only tangible result was the bitterness that enveloped me and the host of confused, frustrated, and often angry people I left behind.

So I stopped. I stopped the committees and the Bible studies, the Sunday school and the missions society. I stopped baking casseroles and sending note cards. I stopped the whirlwind. Funny thing, though, no one seemed to mind. For nearly two years I stopped going to church altogether. I had run myself ragged and ended up dropping out of the race. As my friend Patsy Clairmont says, "I began saying, 'I will be all things to all people.' And ended up saying, 'I'm never doing anything for a fellow human being as long as I live.'"

Have you ever found yourself at that place? Ever wonder how on earth you ended up there? No doubt, you started out with the very best intentions. But rather than bringing you joy and fulfillment, your ministry efforts brought you discouragement and maybe even disillusionment.

I have experienced that time after time in my Christian life. And the conclusion that I've finally come to is this: God has uniquely equipped each of us to run our own race and he promises to help us every step of the way. But he hasn't promised to help us run races he doesn't want us to run. Think about that for a minute. God has uniquely equipped you to run your own race. And he promises to help you every step of the way. But he hasn't promised to help you run races he doesn't want you to run.

You see, all of the great things I wanted to do for God were *my ideas*. In my zeal, I completely neglected to prepare for the race he intended for me. I was running races he didn't want me to run. Are you ready to give up *your* ideas of how you can be of service to God? If so, you're ready to run the race God has set before you.

Take Time to Reflect

1. Have you been running races God doesn't want you to run? In what way?

2. Ask God to give you a vision of the race he wants you to run. Write out a prayer and note any insights that come to your mind/heart.

3. What key lesson did you glean from today's study?

4. Turn to the back of the book and remove your Bible verse card for this week.

Confidence Boosters:

- God has uniquely created you to run your own race and he promises to help you every step of the way.
- God hasn't promised to help you run races he doesn't want you to run.

Day Two

Do We Have To?

Jesus gave them this answer: "I tell you the truth, the Son can do nothing by himself; he can do only what he sees his Father doing"
John 5:19

Yesterday I shared with you some of the "great things" I attempted for God. I also admitted that, even though I was completely sincere, most of these grand endeavors ended with disappointment and confusion. I don't remember when, I don't remember how, but my life changed forever when I finally realized *I don't have to do anything for God.*

Don't panic, you ladies of action! Stick with me here. What I'm saying is this: God doesn't *need* our help. If you'll allow me to borrow a metaphor from my previous book, there's no such thing as a vessel God can't do without. He's the sovereign God of the Universe, thank you very much! God doesn't need our help; he doesn't need our suggestions. Instead, he wants our obedience; he wants our holiness. In his great mercy, he chooses to give us the privilege of participating in his work of redemption on this earth. He allows us the unspeakable honor of being people through whom he can accomplish his eternal agenda. Wow!

Let me throw out a convicting—possibly even scary—thought: too often, when we're busy serving God, what we're really doing is pursuing our own agenda. I know that's what I was doing.

It's almost as if we're saying, "I don't need to consult with God. I know what needs to be done around this church. I know what can be accomplished through my life." Or it may simply be that we're so busy saying yes to people that we have no time or energy to say yes to God. After all, we can't be in two places at the same time. Since

I'm making bold statements, let me take it a step further: Often when we're saying yes to people, we're actually saying no to God.

Picture it like this: there you are, a faithful, hardworking servant teaching Sunday school to little fifth graders. In the beginning, you're excited. You are going to have the greatest class in the history of the church. One problem: the kids don't respond. Then you realize, "Hey, fifth graders are a bit tougher to handle than I thought." But you are a servant of God. You are not going to give up easily! You try harder. You read books on ministering to fifth graders. You buy new materials with your own money. You lie awake at night contemplating ways to reach these kids.

The weird thing is, though, they still don't respond. What's even weirder is those ungrateful parents! Can't they see how hard you're working? What about that thankless Sunday school superintendent? Can you believe he hasn't had a single word of encouragement for you?

Well, the next thing you know you're cursing the day God created fifth graders and singing, "Nobody knows the trouble I've seen." Then you vow you'll never be a servant of the Lord again!

Want to know the real irony?

The whole time you were slaving away with those fifth graders, God was patiently waiting for you to enter into the ministry he intended for you. I can almost hear him clearing his throat and saying, *Um, excuse me, Donna. I can see that you're very busy doing great things for me. And I certainly appreciate that. But if you would set down that burden and step over here for a moment, I have work I want to accomplish through you. Work that I prepared and ordained before the foundation of the world. If you would simply take my yoke upon you, you'd find that it's light and easy. You'd discover that I meant for you to experience the joy and fulfillment that can only come when you yield your life completely to me, when you allow me to accomplish through your life what I've ordained.*

Even Jesus said, "My food is to do the will of Him who sent me and to accomplish *his work*" (John 4:34 RSV, emphasis added). It's not our work we have to do. It's *his work*.

The Christian life is not about "have to's"; it's about "get to's." We *get to* be vessels through whom God can accomplish his purposes here on earth.

I'll say it again: it's not about what we *have to* do for God. It's about how we *get to* be used by him! It's the difference between "working for God" and allowing God to do his work through you. It's the difference between pouring yourself out—and wearing yourself out in the process—and simply allowing the Living Water to pour forth through you.

Do you sense the incredible FREEDOM here?!?!?! Are you sensing the excitement of this? (I'm jumping out of my seat here!) See how that takes all the pressure off and replaces it with joy? See how it eliminates the pressure to perform, the pressure to "win" people to Christ or "advance the kingdom"? God is more than capable of drawing people to himself. He is in charge of advancing his kingdom. Our role is to receive the blessing, to experience the joy of being part of his work.

We GET TO!

It's not a burden! It's a privilege!

I guess if I were to sum it up, I'd say: Forget about the "Rules of the Christian Life" and focus on cultivating your "Relationship With the Living God." That's exactly what the rest of this book is designed to help you do!

Let me close today's session with a quote from Hannah Whitall Smith. Please make this your prayer:

> Here Lord, I abandon myself to you. I have tried in every way I could think of to manage myself and make myself what I know I ought to be. But have always failed. Now I give it up to you. Take entire possession of me. Work in me all the good pleasure of your will. Mold and fashion me into such a vessel as seems good to you. I leave myself in your hands. And I believe you will, according to your promise, make me into a vessel unto your honor, sanctified and meet for the master's use and prepared unto every good work.[1]

Which motto will you choose to live by:

Have to? or Get to?

It's up to you!

---

[1]Hannah Whitall Smith, *The Christian's Secret of a Happy Life* (Springdale, Pa.: Whitaker House, 1983), 96.

Take Time to Reflect

1. As you consider the way you've approached the Christian life, have you lived as one who has to serve God or as one who gets to be used by him?

2. How might your life be different if you moved from "have to" to "get to"?

3. Do you tend to focus more on the "Rules of the Christian Life" or on cultivating "Your Relationship With the Living God"?

4. Which of the above do you think is more important and why?

5. Look up Psalm 32:8 and note God's word of encouragement for you today.

6. Write out a prayer to God, expressing your desire to cultivate your love relationship with him.

7. What key lesson did you glean from today's study?

Confidence Boosters:

- We don't *have to* do anything for God; we *get to* be used by him.
- Focus on cultivating "Your Relationship With the Living God" rather than following the "Rules of the Christian Life."

Day Three

Dream Again

Let's return to our race metaphor to explore how we can "run with perseverance the race marked out *for us*." I emphasized *for us* because I think, too often, we live as if that verse read, "Let us run with perseverance the race marked out *for somebody else.*"

The exciting truth I want you to grab hold of is this: When you run the race God intended for you to run, you suddenly tap into his unlimited power. You tap into a reservoir of strength, wisdom, and enthusiasm that was completely unavailable to you as long as you were "doing your own thing." It will make all the difference in the way you approach ministry and in your ability to run with perseverance the race marked out for you. You will be able to say, with the apostle Paul, that you lived your life holding fast the word of life, so that in the day of Christ you may be proud that you did not run in vain (see Philippians 2:16).

Have you seen the classic movie *Chariots of Fire*? It recounts the true story of 1924 Olympic gold medalist Eric Liddel. You may recall the scene in the movie where Eric and his sister are walking along a cliff in Scotland on a windy afternoon. His sister is trying to persuade him to forget all this frivolous nonsense about running and devote himself to missionary work. She is sincere. She loves her brother and—most of all—she knows God's will for her brother's life. Do you have any people like that around you?

Eric responds with one of the most unforgettable lines. He says, "I know God made me for a purpose. But he made me fast, too. And when I run, I feel God's pleasure."

Eric Liddel goes on to win an Olympic gold medal in such a way that God alone receives all the glory. And afterward, he does indeed become a missionary to China, where he dies at the hands of the Japanese occupying army.

Now let's think about this for a moment. Here is a man whose life inspired an Academy Award-winning movie—a movie that touched the lives of millions of people around the world. Why? Because he died a martyr's death in a Japanese prison camp? No. That wasn't even mentioned in the movie. Why? Because he ran the race God intended him to run.

Is there something you do that, when you do it, you feel God's pleasure? You feel "the smile of God" upon your life? You sense that "Yes, this is it! This is what he created me to do!" I firmly believe that God has a unique calling upon the life of every woman reading this today. He has a role for each of you to fill in your home, in your church, and in your world. And we'll never be fully alive until we put on our running shoes and begin to run the race God has set before us.

I believe this passionately. I remember trying to explain this concept to my daughter Leah, who was about four years old at the time. I said, "Leah, Daddy is a musician. God made him to help us worship and sing praises. Our neighbor Gayle is an interior decorator. God made her to bring beauty into our homes. Now, Leah, what did God make YOU for?" She thought about that for a minute. She wanted to give a good answer. She could *tell* I wanted a good answer. Finally, she looked up at me and said, "Mommy, I think God made me . . . for BOYS."

I'm not sure that story contains profound spiritual significance . . . but I couldn't resist sharing it. Anyway, back to the Bible! Exodus 15:13 offers us an incredible glimpse of God's character: "In your unfailing love you will lead the people you have redeemed." If he has redeemed you, he will lead you. If you feel like you are lacking direction, not really sure where you fit in to God's grand plan, I'd encourage you to think back to when you were a little girl. What did you dream of becoming then? Back when you were eight or nine years old. Back when boys had cooties and we knew that the girls were always smarter. What did you dream? Dare to dream it again, because in counseling with people, I find that those childhood dreams often hold the key to a fulfilling ministry. Just in case you're wondering: When I was a little girl, I dreamed of being a writer and I dreamed of standing on a stage. Funny, I never dreamed of baking casseroles. . . .

I'd also encourage you to reflect on the noble ambitions God laid on your heart when you were a brand-new believer. Remember? In the joy of that moment, what vows did you make before the Lord? Get back in touch with that sense of calling. Then run the race God has chosen for you and delight in feeling his good pleasure.

Take Time to Reflect

1. Is there something you do that, when you do it, you feel God's pleasure? Describe.

2. Can you recall any childhood dreams that might be part of God's call upon your life?

3. Can you recall any noble ambitions you had when you first came to Christ? Might any of these be part of God's call upon your life?

4. Look up Psalm 139:1–10 and note God's word of encouragement for you.

5. Write out a prayer sharing your dreams with God. Ask him if there is a ministry he has for you that you've never even considered.

6. What key lesson did you glean from today's study?

Confidence Boosters:

- God has a unique call upon the life of everyone he redeems. If he has redeemed you, he will lead you.
- You can often discover your unique race by getting back in touch with childhood dreams or the noble ambitions you had as a new believer.

Day Four

God's Will Is Not a Crisis

God's will is not a crisis.
—Dr. David Lindstrom, my former Sunday school teacher

I still remember the day I approached my adult Sunday school class teacher with great trepidation. My husband and I were in the midst of a crisis, or so we thought, and we immediately had to discern God's will for our lives. Cameron was being seriously considered for a major promotion, which would have meant relocating to Washington, D.C. As it happens, I had just been offered my own daily radio show by a ministry based in Arizona. I felt certain God wanted me to have a radio show. I mean, what better way could there be for God to reach the hurting women of America? (It's okay for you to chuckle on that one, but if you roll on the floor with laughter, I might get deeply offended!) Then again, it sure would be nice if my husband got a big pay raise, and if we could get out of the desert and move somewhere with actual trees and green grass.

What on earth were we to do?

As I stood there wringing my hands, clearly ridden with anxiety, my teacher looked at me and said calmly, "God's will is not a crisis."

He was right. And the longer I walk with God, the more convinced I am of just how right he was. I constantly hear people wondering aloud about God's will concerning this or that situation. "Should we buy the blue house on Main Street or the green house on Third Avenue?" Frankly, I'm half convinced that God doesn't particularly care if you get the blue house or the green one. My guess is that he'd advise, "Buy whichever one you like better."

God's will is not a crisis. It's not going to be ruined if you move onto Main Street. His sovereignty extends even that far. What mat-

53

ters is that we seek to glorify him in whatever we do and wherever we live. Ironically, neither the job transfer to Washington nor the radio show ever came to pass.

Let's go back to my favorite runner, Eric Liddel, because once again, he sets a great example. He had trained for many years as a short-distance sprinter. He went to the Olympic Games intending to compete in the 100-meter race, because God had gifted him in that area. More to the point, he firmly believed that God would be glorified when the world realized that the fastest sprinter on earth was a Christian.

God's will didn't unfold quite the way Eric thought it would. Instead, he discovered the trial heat was scheduled to be held on the Sabbath . . . and he was a strict Sabbatarian (that's a fancy word meaning you don't do *anything* on the Lord's Day). Crisis time! What was God's will? Didn't God want him to win the 100-meter race?

Eric must have had an excellent teacher, for he knew that God's will wasn't a crisis. He refused to run. Instead, he entered the 400-meter race, which was scheduled to be run on a weekday. This race was four times the distance he was accustomed to running. It was a race he had never even attempted. Everyone knew he was completely unqualified, so there was no possible way he could win.

When the British Olympic Committee learned of his decision, they were absolutely furious with him. I mean, they didn't know it was going to become an Academy Award-winning movie. All they saw was their great hope of glory dropping out of the race. They called a high-powered meeting, where the Prince of Wales himself tried to persuade Eric Liddel to change his mind. But he stood his ground.

Why? Two very simple reasons. First, he knew that God's will wasn't a crisis. He knew God had a plan, and even though nothing made sense at the moment, he entrusted himself to God. And second, he wasn't running for man's approval. He wasn't running to win a medal or to win a popularity contest. He was serving for God's glory and that made all the difference. And because human approval meant nothing to him, because his eyes were focused heavenward, he conducted himself with quiet confidence—with Total God-Confidence.

If he were competing based on self-confidence, he would have been devastated—or he would have compromised his standards. You will recall that self-confidence takes a little inventory to see what your internal resources are. Then, based on that self-evaluation, you come to some conclusions about what you can or cannot do. Self-confidence looks inward.

God-Confidence looks upward. God-Confidence realizes that it doesn't matter whether or not you're qualified; what matters is whether or not God has called you. God-Confidence knows that God's will isn't a crisis and it isn't something we need to force.

When we live with a sense of calling, confident that God will bring about his plan for our lives, we can truly walk in Total God-Confidence. I would encourage you to rent or buy *Chariots of Fire* and watch it with this in mind: Study the contrast between Eric Liddel, a man who lived with a sense of calling, and Harold Abrahams, the epitome of a driven man. Afterward, ask your heart: Am I living a called or a driven life?

Then if God is calling you to do something, take courage and do it with quiet confidence. "Trust in the Lord with all thine heart; and lean not unto thine own understanding. In all thy ways acknowledge him, and he shall direct thy paths" (Proverbs 3:6, KJV).

Take Time to Reflect

1. Can you recall a time when you acted as if God's will were a crisis? What were the results?

2. Can you recall a time when you acted with quiet confidence? What were the results?

3. Is there a situation you're facing right now that you can choose to respond to with quiet confidence rather than in crisis mode?

4. Look up John 14:27 and note God's word of encouragement for you.

5. Write out a prayer asking God to help you choose his quiet confidence for your life today.

6. What key lesson did you glean from today's study?

Confidence Boosters:

- God's will is not a crisis.
- We can choose to respond to situations in crisis mode or with quiet confidence.
- God is glorified when we live with a sense of calling rather than as one who is driven.

Day Five

When You Fall . . .

I f you'll bear with me through one more Olympic example, I'd like to share with you a story that has forever changed my understanding of who God is; of what it means to be his child.

At the 1982 Summer Olympics in Barcelona, Spain, an event unfolded that captured the imagination of the world. But it wasn't an athlete setting a new world record or winning an unprecedented number of gold medals. When Derek Redmon stepped onto the Olympic track, he had visions of glory in his head. This was the moment he had worked for most of his life. As he took his place among the strongest and fastest runners in the world, all his hopes, all his dreams came down to this one moment in time. In his heart, he knew this was the race he had been created to run.

In the final minutes before the race began, he looked up into the stands and searched for the face of his father. Sure he wanted to win it for himself. But mostly he wanted to win it for his dad. His dad, who had given so much, sacrificed so much to get him to this place. Now he had a chance to do something in return. Now he could make his father proud.

Then the gun went off. Derek took off running, pouring all that he had into the race, ready to run with perseverance the race marked out for him. All was going well until Derek rounded the final turn. Suddenly he collapsed onto the field. He had pulled a hamstring in his leg. He was gripped with incredible pain. He tried to get back up; he tried to hop; but the pain was too much. The seconds seemed like hours as he lay there writhing in pain. He couldn't believe THIS was what his moment of glory had come to.

Perhaps he was worried about what his father might be thinking. Was his father ashamed? Disappointed? Was his father going to turn his back on him and walk away? Was he thinking, *Oh great, all those years* wasted *on one who couldn't even finish the race?*

But, you know, that's not what his father was thinking at all. Up in the stands, his father leaped to his feet. Quickly he began pushing his way through the crowd. By now thousands were standing, gazing at his son, gaping at the spectacle of his son's suffering. Finally, he made his way to the edge of the Olympic track. A security guard stopped him and said, "No one is allowed on the track."

Derek's father responded with three simple words: "That's my son."

He would not be held back. He moved past the security guard and went out onto the track. And as thousands roared their approval, he walked his son over the finish line.

Maybe some of you feel like you have fallen. You want to finish the race God has set before you but the pain is too much. No matter how hard you try, you can't seem to get back on your feet. Maybe you're afraid your heavenly Father is disappointed in you, that he is not pleased.

I have spent most of my Christian life trying to run the race in such a way that God would approve of me. But time and time again, I would fall. In my heart and in my mind, I saw God sitting in the stands with his arms folded, disappointed and disapproving. I never really understood before that God is on my side . . . but I'm beginning to.

Do you know that God is on your side? God is not disappointed in you when you stumble. You are his precious daughter! You are your heavenly Daddy's little girl. Oh, when you stumble how it grieves him. How he feels for you. *God is for you.* He wants you to finish the race and he will do everything he can to get you across that finish line. Even if it means carrying you across.

Perhaps some of you don't even know your heavenly Father. But he is there waiting for you. He longs to embrace you as his precious daughter and to guide you, every step of the way, as you run the race of life. The only way to come to the Father is through his Son. Jesus said, "No one comes to the Father except through me" (John 14:6 NIV).

I don't know about the rest of you, but I can't think of anything that gives me more comfort than this: The very one who calls us to run the race is the one who helps us over the finish line.

Take Time to Reflect

1. Describe your reaction to today's story:

2. If you are unsure about your relationship with the heavenly Father, please turn to the "Steps to Freedom" in the back of the book.

3. Write out a prayer expressing your heartfelt thanks to the God who is on your side.

4. What key lesson did you glean from today's study?

5. Write out This Week's Verse from memory.

Confidence Boosters:

- God is on your side.
- The very one who calls you to run the race is the one who helps you over the finish line.

Weekly Review:

See if you can fill in the ten characteristics of walking in Total God-Confidence. Look in the back of the book if you need help.

C_____ according to his purpose

O_____ to his plan

N_____ by his love

F_____ from the chains that bind

I _____ conformed to his character

D_____ in his Word

E_____ by faith

N_____ shaken by the jerks

C_____ that he is able and faithful

E _____ to take the leap of faith

WEEK THREE:

Nourished by His Love

This Week's Verse:

How great is the love the father has lavished on us, that we
should be called children of God!
And that is what we are!

1 John 1:3 (NIV)

Day One

Princess With an Attitude (PWA)

I want to share with you one of my favorite verses in the Bible:

> *How great is the love the Father has lavished on us, that we should be called children of God! And that is what we are!*
>
> 1 John 3:1 NIV

You may not know this, but there are certain verses in the Bible that only work if you read them *with an attitude!* Okay, I want you to stand up. Come on, stand up. Read through the verse again, but this time read it aloud. When you get to the part that says, "And that is what we are!" I want you to put your hands on your hips and say it *with attitude.* I mean, a "don't even mess with me" attitude!

(We have to do this in person sometime! It'll be lots more fun.)

Let's think about the implications of this verse for a minute: If God is the King and you are his daughter, what does that make you? A PRINCESS. But no ordinary princess. A Princess With an Attitude. We're talking PWA! This PWA stuff wasn't an afterthought. Not a side-benefit. Oh no. Ephesians 1:4–6 tells us that bestowing the princess title upon us was God's plan from the very beginning: "In love he predestined us to be adopted as his [daughters] through Jesus Christ." And why did he come up with such a neat plan? ". . . in accordance with his pleasure and will—to the praise of his glorious grace, which he has freely given us in the One he loves."

I'll never forget speaking at a retreat where the average attendee was about seventy and the oldest was in her nineties. It was a bit awkward the first night, because it was pretty obvious that I was just a fraction of their age. I challenged them to consider that maybe, just maybe, God was big enough to work through a *young, slightly wacky vessel.* They were a bit skeptical, but once we got to the PWA part, we bonded! Hey, a princess is a princess, regardless of her age.

That night a group of ladies broke into the camp kitchen and raided the aluminum foil. I thought I would die when they showed up the next morning in the front row with their aluminum foil tiaras. What fun! That's the kind of princess I want to be as I approach my centennial.

But don't go crazy on me, now! (When I send women home from a ladies' retreat, I almost feel sorry for their families! In comes Mom with a giant aluminum foil tiara and an attitude the size of a football player!) I don't mean a cocky attitude. I mean a God-Confident attitude. An attitude that says, "I know who I am and I walk accordingly."

Those of you with teenagers have probably heard the expression "Talk to the hand!" (They put their hand right in your face when they say it!) It means, "There's nothing negative you've got to say to me that I'm gonna hear." Well, when the enemy comes against us, we need to say, "Talk to the hand! Don't even mess with me, 'cause I'm a princess. Talk to the Nail-Scarred Hand. The hand that bled to earn for me the *right* to be called a child of God."

Wasn't that PWA stuff fun? But some of you are thinking, "There's still one problem. Now I know I'm a princess, *but my family still thinks I'm a HAG.*"

Well, that is a bit of a problem, but it isn't insurmountable. Just keep believing the truth about yourself and eventually they'll catch on. I love the story of *The Little Princess* by Frances Hodgson Burnett. You may recall the tale of an aristocratic little girl who leaves her luxurious home in India to attend a ritzy boarding school in England. When her father dies, she experiences a reversal of fortune. Rather than living in splendor, dressed in the finest clothes, she's reduced to poverty and rags. However, regardless of how deplorably she is treated, she always conducts herself like a little princess. Despite her bedraggled appearance, eventually everyone must acknowledge the truth: she is still a princess at heart.

Remember that a princess always conducts herself like a princess, regardless of her circumstances.

Practically speaking, how do we conduct ourselves like princesses in the face of trials? How do we become our real selves: those radiant princesses God intended us to be? Here's how Andrew Murray puts it:

In time of trouble say,
First, he brought me here. It is by his will I am in this place, in
that will I rest.
Next, he will keep me in his love and give me grace in this trial
to behave as his child.
Then, he will make the trial a blessing, teaching me the lessons
he means me to learn, and working in me the grace he intends
for me.
Last, in his good time, he can bring me out again, how and when
only he knows.
Say, I am here:
By God's appointment,
In God's keeping,
Under his training,
For his time.
—from *Humility*[1]

Now that's PWA! Isn't it? Nothing can shake a princess who lives
like that. A princess who says, "This is where I am, so this must be
where God wants me. He is taking care of me, even if other people
don't think he's doing a very good job of it. He's teaching me, preparing me for a special assignment that right now I can't even fathom.
But I'll be faithful each day, so when the opportunity comes to reign
like the true princess I am, I'll be ready."

No matter what your circumstances, walk like a princess.

Know who you are! You're a PWA!

The following poem was given to me at a retreat, typed up on a
bookmark. I wish I knew who wrote it! If you're out there and you
read this, please don't mind my changing the last word from King to
PRINCESS! Let's make this the PWA creed:

The Crown That I Wear

The crown that I wear
does not tarnish;
It's not made
of worldly ores.

---

[1]Andrew Murray, *Humility* (reprint) (Fort Washington, Pa.: Christian Literature Crusade, 1993).

I don't need to polish
and store it
In a vault
or behind metal doors.
The crown is a gift
from my Father
Whose Son died so that I
could be free.
What an honor it is
just to wear it,
For His last thoughts
on earth were of me.
The crown has
a special meaning;
It's not about worldly success.
It stands for the
The love of my Lord
and Savior,
Which I wear everyday
like a Princess.

Take Time to Reflect

1. Do you believe, in your heart, that you are a princess? How does
   your life reflect what you believe?

2. What circumstances have caused you to doubt that you really are
   a princess?

3. What are some practical ways you can walk as a PWA, despite your circumstances?

4. Write out a prayer thanking the King for adopting you into his kingdom.

5. What key lesson did you glean from today's study?

6. Turn to the back of the book and remove your Bible verse card for this week.

Confidence Boosters:

- Since God is our father and he is the King, that makes each and every one of us a princess!
- A princess always conducts herself like a princess, regardless of her circumstances.

Day Two

The Unlikely Princess

> *Rahab, the prostitute, is another example of this. She was saved because of what she did when she hid those messengers and sent them safely away by a different road.*　　　　James 2:25

Princesses come in all different shapes and sizes. They come in every color of the rainbow, from every country on this spinning globe. And they come from the most unusual backgrounds.

Did you ever wonder what happens up in heaven when God decides he needs a princess through whom to accomplish his purposes on earth? I did an extensive study on this, through the Bible and all of church history. Do you know what I discovered? When God wants to intervene in human history, he looks down upon the earth and chooses . . . THE WRONG PERSON.

Let me give you an example. The Israelites had wandered through the desert for forty years, after being in bondage for 400 years. Finally, they were ready to enter the Promised Land. But God needed someone to play a key role in this historical moment. This was a big moment. I mean, Cecil B. DeMille big. So, he searched the world over and picked . . . a PROSTITUTE.

Is that who you would have picked? Be honest.

Let's pick up the story in the second chapter of Joshua:

> *Then Joshua sent two spies from the Israeli camp at Acacia to cross the river and check out the situation on the other side, especially at Jericho. They arrived at an inn operated by a woman named Rahab, who was a prostitute. They were planning to spend the night there, but someone informed the king of Jericho that two Israelis who were suspected of being spies had arrived in the city that evening. He dispatched a police squadron to Rahab's home,*

demanding that she surrender them. "They are spies," he explained. "They have been sent by the Israeli leaders to discover the best way to attack us." But she had hidden them, so she told the officer in charge, "The men were here earlier, but I didn't know they were spies. They left the city at dusk as the city gates were about to close, and I don't know where they went. If you hurry you can probably catch up with them!" But actually she had taken them up to the roof and hidden them beneath piles of flax that were drying there. (vv. 1–7)

Has the president of the United States ever sent a contingent of marines to your front door? If they gave you a specific command, would you have the guts to defy them? Rahab did. She turned her back on her king and her country. She risked her life to rescue the spies. The question is why. Were they just such irresistibly sweet men that she wanted to lend them a hand? Or were they so impressive that she thought these two wonder-guys could protect her from an entire nation?

I don't think either of those explanations make sense. I don't even think she trusted them. I mean, as a rule, do you think prostitutes trust men? Not likely. Her actions had absolutely nothing to do with those men and everything to do with her faith and trust in God. Don't take my word for it, though. Look at her declaration of faith:

Rahab went up to talk to the men before they retired for the night. "I know perfectly well that your God is going to give my country to you," she told them. (vv. 8–9)

Now that's a woman with Total God-Confidence. There's not a shadow of a doubt in her mind that God will give the Israelites the Promised Land, no matter what it takes. If you know anything at all about the Old Testament, you will recall that's a lot more than most of the Israelites believed. In fact, the whole reason they'd been wandering around in the wilderness for forty years was because they *didn't* believe. Rahab believed. God said he would do it, and she considered it as good as done. She tells us the basis of her belief in verse 11: "for your God is the supreme God of heaven, not just an ordinary god."

Even though Rahab was born and raised in a pagan country, surrounded by idols, she had better theology than most of the Israelites. If you doubt that, read the book of Judges and see for yourself. If we want to walk in Total God-Confidence like Princess Rahab, we need to follow her lead:

- Take God at his Word. If God has said something, you can consider it as good as done. Call to mind a specific promise, either from God's Word or something he has personally promised you in accordance with his Word, and decide that you'll believe it, come what may.
- Go against the crowd. If you're on God's side (notice I didn't say if he's on yours, but if you are on his!), then you can stand firm, even though a million people oppose you. Can you think of even one area of your life where you are going against the crowd? If not, perhaps you are being conformed to this world, rather than being transformed by the renewing of your mind (Romans 12:2).
- If you believe God is calling you to do something, then do something about it. Talk is cheap, so put some feet to your faith. Can you think of a specific action you can take, today, by faith?

Take Time to Reflect

1. Do you take God at his Word? Give an example of an area of your life where you are taking God at his Word.

2. Can you name a single area of your life where you are going against the crowd? If not, do you think that says something about your degree of God-Confidence?

3. What one action did you decide to take by faith?

4. Look up Hebrews 11:1 and note God's word of encouragement for you.

5. Write out a prayer asking God to give you an infusion of God-Confidence.

6. What key lesson did you glean from today's study?

Confidence Boosters:

- Take God at his Word.
- Be willing to go against the crowd.
- Put feet to your faith.

Day Three

Awaiting the Rescue

I will never worship anyone but you! For how can I thank you enough for all you have done? I will surely fulfill my promises. For my deliverance comes from the Lord alone.   Jonah 2:9

Today we continue our study of Princess Rahab. Her encounter with the Hebrew spies concludes with a promise:

"Now I beg for this one thing: Swear to me by the sacred name of your God that when Jericho is conquered you will let me live, along with my father and mother, my brothers and sisters, and all their families. This is only fair after the way I have helped you." The men agreed. "If you won't betray us, we'll see to it that you and your family aren't harmed," they promised. "We'll defend you with our lives." Then, since her house was on top of the city wall, she let them down by a rope from a window. . . . But before they left, the men had said to her, "We cannot be responsible for what happens to you unless this rope is hanging from this window and unless all your relatives—your father, mother, brothers, and anyone else— are here inside the house. . . ." "I accept your terms," she replied. And she left the scarlet rope hanging from the window.
                                                    (Joshua 2:12–18, 21)

It's significant to note that Rahab's house was located on the city wall. That meant that when the Israelites came to conquer, she would have a bird's-eye view of all the action. By faith, Rahab put the scarlet cord (which, incidentally, is a symbol of trusting in Christ's blood for deliverance) in her window, then watched and waited for God to deliver her.

She did have other options. She could have fled the city. She didn't. She didn't develop a contingency plan. She didn't try to extricate herself from a difficult situation. No, God said he would deliver. So, she sat waiting upon him. How about you? Are you in a tough situation right now? Are you tempted to deliver yourself?

Follow Rahab's example. She walked in Total God-Confidence. (Well, actually, she *sat* in Total God-Confidence.) Can't you just picture her, sitting in her window on the city wall, watching for God to come rescue her? Pretty exciting stuff!

At last the big day comes and Rahab sees the army of the Lord marching toward Jericho. She's ready for the big deliverance. The army comes and they . . . walk around the block.

What?

Yep, they just walk around the city.

This isn't exactly how she thought this "mighty deliverance" would unfold, but that's okay. Tomorrow's another day.

Day 2. Rahab's ready for the big deliverance, and the army of the Lord . . . walks around the block.

Rahab must have thought to herself, *Hmmm, this is getting weird. Maybe I should have moved to Egypt with Uncle Ahab. But I'm not gonna panic. Maybe God will deliver me tomorrow. . . .*

Day 3. *This is it, for sure. He's not gonna make me wait another day.* And the army of the Lord . . . walks around the block.

Okay, okay. Very funny. Just my luck, I think I finally meet God, I think I'm finally getting out of this stinking town, out of this miserable lifestyle. And what does God do? Nada. *I should've known nothing good would ever happen to me. But, well, maybe tomorrow.*

Day 4. The army of the Lord . . . walks around the block.

All right, this is ridiculous. I'm trying to walk by faith here, God. Well, actually, I'm trying to sit by faith, but you know what I'm talking about. I can't believe you did this to me. I should have known you'd never save a wretch like me. My mom was right. I don't matter to anyone. Even God lies to me. But, you did SAY you'd rescue me . . . didn't you say that, God? I could have sworn I distinctly heard you say that. Maybe tomorrow. . . .

Day 5. *This is ludicrous. I should have gotten out of here while the getting was good.*

Day 6. *I will never, never, never trust anyone again. Not you, God, not anyone. I've had it. I get my hopes up, for what? To be crushed underfoot again.*

Day 7. The army marches around the city once. Twice. Three times. Four. Five. Six. Seven. The trumpets blast. At that moment, the entire wall crashes to the ground—except the home of Rahab the prostitute. She folds her arms in satisfaction and mumbles, *Yeah, I never doubted for a minute.*

God has promised to deliver you, too. The question is, are you willing to wait—with Total God-Confidence—for his deliverance? You'll never see what God can do until you let go of what you can do.

The story of Rahab, the Most Unlikely Princess, gets even better. You see, God met her where she was, in a house of prostitution, but he loved her too much to leave her there. Instead, he invited her to go forward with him. Joshua 6:25 tells us that "she lives among the Israelites to this day." God actually allowed her to enter into the Promised Land as one of his chosen people.

But the story gets even better. If you turn to the very first page of the New Testament, you'll find the Most Unlikely Princess waiting for us there: "Salmon was the father of Boaz (Rahab was his mother)" (Matthew 1:5).

Can you believe it? She actually became one of the grandmothers of Jesus? Our favorite princess even earns honorable mention in the Great Hall of Faith:

> *By faith—because she believed in God and his power—Rahab the harlot did not die with all the others in her city when they refused to obey God, for she gave a friendly welcome to the spies.* (Hebrews 11:31)

Do you think you're *the* Most Unlikely Princess in the world? Nope, the honor has already been taken! But if you'd like to join a parade of MUPPETS (get it? Most Unlikely Princess-ets), we've still got room in the group. Put on your aluminum foil tiara and join us!

Take Time to Reflect

1. Are you facing a situation, right now, from which you need deliverance? Describe.

2. What types of contingency plans have you set up? How have you tried to deliver yourself?

3. Are you willing to wait on God for deliverance? How can you demonstrate that willingness in a tangible way (remember the scarlet cord)?

4. Do you think of yourself as one of the MUPPETS (Most Unlikely Princesses)? Why?

5. Look up Exodus 33:13–14 and note God's word of encouragement for you.

6. Write out a prayer inviting God to transform you into one of his MUPPETS. (Be prepared for some great new adventures.)

7. What key lesson did you glean from today's study?

Confidence Boosters:

- God chooses the Most Unlikely Princesses!
- If you need a deliverer, wait on God. Don't try to deliver yourself.

Day Four

Cultivating Your Love Relationship

Jesus replied: "Love the Lord your God with all your heart and with all your soul and with all your mind. This is the first and greatest commandment."　　　　　Matthew 22:37–38 NIV

Do you know Christians who have a rule for everything? Rules about music, about dancing, about movies? Rules about relationships and religious days? I do. I feel sorry for them. They've lost sight of what the Gospel, the Good News, is all about. Apparently the apostle Paul had some friends who were falling into the same trap. In his letter to the Galatian believers he wrote:

"You foolish Galatians! Who has bewitched you? Before your very eyes Jesus Christ was clearly portrayed as crucified. I would like to learn just one thing from you: Did you receive the Spirit by observing the law, or by believing what you heard? Are you so foolish? After beginning with the Spirit, are you now trying to attain your goal by human effort? . . . .

"But now that you know God—or rather are known by God—how is it that you are turning back to those weak and miserable principles? Do you wish to be enslaved by them all over again? You are observing special days and months and seasons and years! I fear for you, that somehow I have wasted my efforts on you" (Galatians 3:1–3; 4:9–10 NIV).

The Good News is that, through Christ, we are daughters of the King. Princesses have direct access to their Father, the King. We no longer need to approach him through the Law. Rather than living by a set of rules, we live by faith. The heart of the Christian life is not rules, but a love relationship with the living God.

I don't know about the rest of you, but I have a limited supply of time and energy. I figure, any moment I spend concentrating on lists is time that would be better spent cultivating my love relationship with God.

Here's how Henry Blackaby, author of *Experiencing God*, puts it:

> Everything in your Christian life, everything about knowing Him and experiencing Him, everything about knowing His will, depends on the quality of your love relationship to God. If that is not right, nothing in your life will be right.[1]

Did God choose Princess Rahab because she lived by the right set of rules? Or because he saw that her heart was open to a love relationship with him? Do you think that when God asked Rahab to join him in his work, she responded, "I can't believe I have to serve God. That means I can't go see that new movie that's playing at the Jericho Cinema"? No. Princess Rahab was overjoyed to be entering into a relationship with God. She was surely thrilled that she "got to" be used by him.

I think the following beautifully summarizes what it means to have a loving relationship with your heavenly Father:

> Childlike confidence makes us pray as none else can. It causes a man to pray for great things that he would never have asked for if he had not learned this confidence. It also causes him to pray for little things that many people are afraid to ask for, because they have not yet felt toward God the confidence of children. I have often felt that it requires more confidence in God to pray to Him about a little thing than about great things. We imagine that our great things are somehow worthy of God's attention, though in truth they are little enough to Him. And then we think that our little things must be so insignificant that it is an insult to bring them before Him. We need to realize that what is very important to a child may be very small to his parent, and yet the parent measures the thing not from his own point of view but from the child's. You heard your little boy the other day crying bitterly. The cause of the pain was a splinter in his finger. While you did not call in three surgeons to extract it, the splinter

---

[1] Henry Blackaby, *Experiencing God* (Baptist Sunday School Board Publication, 1990), 34.

was a great thing to that little sufferer. Standing there with eyes all wet through tears of anguish, it never occurred to that boy that his pain was too small a thing for you to care about. What were mothers and fathers made for but to look after the small concerns of little children? And God our Father is a good father who pities us as fathers pity their children. He counts the stars and calls them all by name, yet he heals the broken in heart and binds up their wounds.[2]

What's the status of your love relationship with the King? He invites you to enter his private throne room and spend time getting acquainted with him. He wants you to bring him all of your concerns, both small and large.

Make it your earnest prayer that the heart of your Christian experience would be a vital, living relationship with God, rather than good doctrine and a list of rules.

Take Time to Reflect

1. Is the heart of your Christian experience a list of rules or a relationship with the living God?

2. The King invites you, as his princess, to enter into his throne room and spend time with him. How often do you accept the invitation?

---

[2]Charles Spurgeon, compiled and edited by Robert Hall, *The Power of Prayer in a Believer's Life* (Lynnwood, Wash.: Emerald Books, 1993), 104.

3. Write out a prayer thanking the King for giving you an open invitation to his throne room.

4. What key lesson did you glean from today's study?

Confidence Boosters:

- The Christian life is not a list of rules; it's a relationship with the living God.
- The King invites you, as his princess, to enter into his throne room and spend time with him.
- If you want to live like a princess, spend time with royalty.

Day Five

Listen With Your Heart

I want you to come with me, in your imagination, to witness an extraordinary event. It's the Dipsea Competition, a race held in that part of Northern California where the giant redwoods grow. I want you to imagine hundreds of runners, racing up one side of a giant mountain, then down it to the edge of the sea. Realize that simply walking up the mountain is a challenge, let alone trying to *run* up and down it.

Now I want you to bring to mind two men in the midst of the many. They are running the race side-by-side, arm-in-arm because one man is blind and the other can see. The blind man clings closely to his seeing friend, listening intently for his voice. The seeing man calls out words of warning, like "root" or "rock." He also calls words of encouragement.

The blind man does not dare attempt any part of the race apart from his companion. He knows full well there's no other way he can make it to that finish line. No matter how talented, how sincere, how determined he may be, without the help of someone who can see the course, he simply cannot finish the race.

Do you know that God wants you to run the race of life just like that blind man? Arm-in-arm, listening intently for his voice? Not daring to take a step until you've heard from him first? Indeed, the very essence of the Christian life is that "we live by faith, not by sight" (2 Corinthians 5:7).

Isaiah 30:21 promises, "Whether you turn to the right or to the left, your ears will hear a voice behind you, saying, 'This is the way; walk in it.'" The simple truth is, if you are not listening for God's voice, you cannot run the race. If you are not in a close, loving relationship with God, you cannot live the Christian life effectively. You may be sincere. You may be enthusiastic. You may be bound and determined. You may even have great doctrine and believe all the right things about God. But only God can see.

So, is listening for those instructions a simple matter? I have to confess, I was tempted to include here "The Four Surefire Ways to Hear God's Voice." It's not that simple. It's a lifelong process of learning how to listen. And I've noticed that sometimes God intentionally whispers to cause us to listen more intently. At other times, he's screaming at the top of his lungs, throwing roadblocks in front of us, but we refuse to listen.

Whatever the case may be, one truth is certain: God is not in the business of keeping secrets. He is not sitting on his heavenly throne with his arms folded, saying, "You gals figure it out for yourselves."

God is always speaking in a myriad of ways: through his Word, through prayer, through other believers, and even through your circumstances. The question is: are you listening?

Jesus is our example. You never get the sense that he was running ragged. His public ministry lasted only three years, yet he was able to say, in speaking with the Father, "I have COMPLETED the work you gave me to do" (emphasis added). As moms, wouldn't it be nice, just once, to say, "Yes, I have completed the work. The laundry has been finished once and for all." Although, I have said to my family a few times, "I AM finished!"

Notice the difference between the work *other people* wanted Jesus to do and the work *his Father* gave him to do. Two very different things. Plenty of blind men remained blind. Plenty of sick people remained sick. Many died and were not raised from the dead, as Lazarus was. So how did Jesus know? How did Jesus know which needs to meet and which to leave unmet? The same way we can know: by listening to the Father's voice.

God is speaking. He is longing to cultivate a close love relationship with you. Are you listening?

Take Time to Reflect

1. Are you listening? Pick up a pen and pray, "Speak Lord, for your servant listens" (1 Samuel 3:10). Write his response here:

2. What key lesson did you glean from today's study?

3. Write out This Week's Verse from memory.

Confidence Boosters:

- Without the help of the One who can see the course, you simply cannot run the race.
- God is always speaking in a myriad of ways. The question is: Are you listening?

Weekly Review:

See if you can fill in the ten characteristics of walking in Total God-Confidence. Look in the back of the book if you need help.

C _____ according to his purpose

O _____ to his plan

N _____ by his love

F _____ from the chains that bind

I _____ conformed to his character

D _____ in his Word

E _____ by faith

N _____ shaken by the jerks

C _____ that he is able and faithful

E _____ to take the leap of faith

WEEK FOUR:
Free From the Chains That Bind

This Week's Verse:

It is for freedom that Christ has set us free. Stand firm, then,
and do not let yourselves be burdened again by
a yoke of slavery.

Galatians 5:1 (NIV)

Day One

The Elephants Are Coming

If the Son therefore shall make you free, ye shall be free indeed.
John 8:36 KJV

My sister collects thimbles. My daughter Nikki collects angels. My daughter Leah collects everything: stones, feathers, butterflies, stuffed animals, you name it. Me? I don't collect anything. That's because I know that if I collect it, it will collect dust. Then I'll have to clean it and that sounds too much like work!

That's why I was caught off guard about a year ago when . . . the elephants started coming. Stuffed elephants, elephant earrings, an elephant belt, even an elephant planter. Mind you, I didn't go looking for this stuff; it came looking for me. Every time I turned around, another elephant was marching into my life.

Well, I've been a Christian long enough to know that maybe, just maybe, God was trying to get a message through to me. After all, if God could speak through Balaam's donkey (Numbers 22), he could speak through elephants. So I began thinking about it. "Okay, Lord, what are you trying to tell me? Go easy on the Oreos maybe?"

But I knew that a God of love would never send a message like that! Then I heard the story of captive elephants. Have you ever been to a circus and observed a giant elephant with a small rope around its ankle? Did you ever stop to think, "Hey, wait a minute. Technically speaking, there is no way that dinky little rope can hold back that giant elephant!" Did you ever wonder how it came to pass that a giant elephant is held in place by something that has no power to contain him?

Here's how it works. When trainers begin taming a baby elephant, they place a giant chain around its ankle and stake it into the ground.

Day after day, hour after hour, the baby elephant struggles to escape. But his efforts are in vain. He simply cannot break free from the grip of that powerful chain. Eventually, he surrenders. He resolves in his mind that there is no possible way he can escape that chain. So, he relinquishes forever the struggle to be free.

And so it happens that ten, twenty, thirty years later, the giant elephant remains held in bondage by something that really has NO POWER to control him. When I first heard that story, a voice cried out within me, *Donna, that's you! You're allowing your life to be controlled by things that no longer have the power to control you.*

Is it true of you, too?

The apostle Paul wrote, "It is for freedom that Christ has set us free. Stand firm then, and do not let yourselves be burdened again by a yoke of slavery" (Galatians 5:1 NIV).

When Christ went to the Cross, he broke the chains that bind us. He set us free from the power of sin and death. If you have trusted Christ for your salvation, you're no longer in bondage: "For if you tell others with your own mouth that Jesus Christ is your Lord, and believe in your own heart that God has raised him from the dead, you will be saved" (Romans 10:9).

If you have *not* taken that step of faith, the chains are *real*. You're like that baby elephant who literally cannot escape. You cannot escape the penalty for your sins nor can you escape the guilt, fear, and shame that haunt those who haven't made things right with their Creator. At the back of this book, you'll find "Steps to Freedom." If you have any doubts about where you stand—free or in bondage—I would urge you to turn there now. Think and pray about the passages and truths presented. If you are part of a weekly study group, talk to your discussion leader and make sure you get connected with a solid, Bible-teaching church.

Okay, let's assume that's resolved. You have been set free in Christ and therefore the *chains* have been broken. You've been set free to live free. If you're not *living free*, it's probably because you (or someone else) has tied some dinky little rope around your ankle. Since you haven't taken a close enough look, you're giving that rope far more power than it deserves.

Usually the rope is some type of fear: fear of failure, fear of success, fear of rejection, etc. Examine your rope. Name the fear, and remember that perfect love, which is the love we have in Christ, casts out fear. "There is no fear in love. But perfect love drives out fear" (1 John 4:18 NIV).

Throughout this week, I want you to ponder: "Am I still living like I'm in chains? Lord, show me how. Give me the courage to shake my foot loose and walk away in Total God-Confidence, knowing I've been set free and called according to your purpose."

I pray that many who are reading these words will enter into a new sense, a deeper reality, of the freedom we have in Christ.

Take Time to Reflect

1. Are you, in some way, like that giant elephant held in bondage by a rope? Describe.

2. Can you think of something you would do, right now, if you were truly free?

3. Look up Psalm 119:45 and note God's word of encouragement for you.

4. What is it that's holding you back? Identify your "rope," your fear. Write out a prayer, that God's love will cast it out!

5. What key lesson did you glean from today's study?

6. Turn to the back of the book and remove your Bible verse card for this week.

Confidence Boosters:

- We have been set free to *live* free.
- Don't let fear hold you back from being/doing all God has in mind for you. Remember, perfect love casts out fear.

Day Two

Set Free From the Approval Trap

When I consider the chains that have bound me, nothing has been more powerful than my yearning for human approval. More precisely, it has been my fear that I would *not* receive approval and would be rejected. All my life, I've struggled to break free from feeling like "the kid no one was allowed to play with."

Even though I clearly heard God's call to ministry, I figured it was better not to try at all than to try and have people laugh at me, scorn me, or reject me. My fears controlled me as long as I focused on *people's response* rather than *God's request*.

Are you in bondage to people's opinions of you? Have you fallen into what I call the Approval Trap? You'll know you've fallen into the Approval Trap when you find yourself performing to earn applause rather than serving to glorify God.

Jesus specifically warned his disciples against this trap: "How can you believe if you accept praise from one another, yet make no effort to obtain the praise that comes from the only God?" (John 5:44 NIV). Too often, we seek glory from one another and that's why we become frustrated in our Christian walk.

I think that when we enter into ministry—whether it's to our own family, reaching out to a neighbor, teaching Sunday school, leading a women's Bible study, or serving in the church nursery—we have to constantly examine our motives. I know I do. Are you performing to earn applause or serving for God's glory? Since we're human, none of our motives will ever be completely pure.

But I can tell you one thing I've learned the hard way: if approval is the motivating force behind our efforts, it is a trap. Why? Because what happens when we don't get the approval we were hoping for? It opens up the floodgates of sin. We're talking floodgates. The kind of sins that entangle us so easily: bitterness, anger, resentment, jealousy, self-pity; the list goes on. The kind of sins the Bible specifically tells us we need to *throw off*:

> *Therefore, since we are surrounded by such a great cloud of witnesses, let us throw off everything that hinders and the sin that so easily entangles, and let us run with perseverance the race marked out for us. Let us fix our eyes on Jesus, the author and perfecter of our faith, who for the joy set before him endured the cross, scorning its shame, and sat down at the right hand of the throne of God. Consider him who endured such opposition from sinful men, so that you will not grow weary and lose heart. (Hebrews 12:1–3 NIV)*

Do you want to know when you will be free, truly free to walk in Total God-Confidence? The day you learn to pronounce the letters, N-O. For some reason, we can do a sensational job of that as toddlers, but the minute a woman reaches maturity, she just can't seem to say the word. And do you know why? Very simple reason. WE WANT APPROVAL. That immediate human feedback means more, is more real to us, than the eternal reward God has promised to those who will run the race *he* has set before them. A good rule of thumb is this: Say YES to the burden God has placed on your heart and NO to everything else.

Here's a little test you can give yourself the next time you're considering any ministry opportunity. Ask yourself: CAN I DO THIS WITHOUT EXPECTING ANYTHING IN RETURN? Whether it's a thank-you note, applause, to become special friends with the person who asked you, or a wing in the church named after you. If you expect anything at all, other than to hear from your Master's lips, "Well done, good and faithful servant!" (Matthew 25:21 NIV), don't do it. Because if God is truly calling you, HIS approval will be enough.

I'd like to share with you a time in my life when I fell deep into the Approval Trap. So deep, in fact, I didn't think I'd ever get back out again. I shared with you how Nikki came to live with us, how I felt it was God's plan for us. What I didn't mention, what I didn't even admit to myself at the time, was that I had a hidden motive: I wanted approval. In my heart, I was thinking, *Hey, this girl will go from being homeless to living with me. She's going to idolize me. And when her life is transformed, everyone will marvel at my parenting skills. She'll tell everyone in my church and everyone in my neighborhood how wonderful her life is now that she's living with DONNA PARTOW!*

It didn't quite work out that way.

Instead, she found my hot button. Remember what it is? Nothing strikes terror into my heart faster than feeling like "the girl in the neighborhood that nobody wants to play with." So off she went, telling anyone who would listen what a horrible person I was. How her life used to be so wonderful (what?!?!), but now had become a living nightmare. She told wild stories about people frantically screaming at each other on Sunday mornings, then getting to the church parking lot in time to smile and say, "Praise the Lord." (I don't know how she came up with that one. My home is completely peaceful and harmonious on Sunday mornings . . . isn't yours? Hmmm.)

This was not leading to the approval I was hoping for!

I can tell this story humorously now, but at the time, I was dying inside. I felt so . . . so . . . well, TRAPPED. I can remember turning to my husband and saying, in essence, "We've got to throw this kid overboard. She's hurting my reputation. This could damage my illustrious ministry. I mean, we've got to hurry up and do some damage control here."

I can even more vividly remember the moment God backed me up against the wall, put his finger in my face and declared, "This isn't a project. This is a person!"

Uh-oh.

Well, Nikki still lives with us. She doesn't always approve of me, but I do believe her life has brought—and will continue to bring— glory to God. What else could possibly matter?

When we enter into ministry with wrong motives, when we're striving for human approval, we develop a project mentality. We forget that we're messing with human lives.

I've got a new Golden Rule: If I can't serve for God's glory, I stay home. Why not adopt it as your own?

Take Time to Reflect

1. Can you recall a time when you were performing to earn applause rather than serving for God's glory? Describe.

2. What were the results?

3. Look up Philippians 4:4–9 and note God's word of encouragement.

4. Write out a prayer asking God to help you serve for his glory *alone*.

5. What key lesson did you glean from today's study?

Confidence Boosters:

- Before performing any act of service, ask yourself: Can I do this without expecting anything in return?
- Ask your heart: Am I serving for God's glory or performing to earn human applause and approval?
- If God is truly calling you, his approval will be enough.

Day Three

Escaping the Approval Trap

Okay, how many of you are like me? Here's how my mind works: *I won't go into this with wrong motives, no sir. I'll do this just for God's glory. But since I'm working so hard for God with such pure motives, surely he'll send me that approval stuff as a bonus!*

What? No one else thinks that way? Yeah, right!

The fact is, we can be smack-dab in the center of God's will and be showered with human disapproval. In our culture, my guess is that the closer you are to the center of God's will, the *less* approval you'll get.

Today we're going to examine an extended passage from God's Word. You can draw some of your own conclusions, but I couldn't resist throwing in my comments for good measure. Let me paint the scenario: Nehemiah and a group of Israelites have been released from Babylonian captivity by the Persian king and given permission to rebuild Jerusalem. Nehemiah's motives are as pure as the driven snow and the task he has undertaken is clearly one intended to glorify God. Raise your hand if you bet he gets lots of approval for his efforts. Now read the story:

> *Sanballat* [some local political hot shot] *was very angry when he learned that we were rebuilding the wall. He flew into a rage, and insulted and mocked us and laughed at us, and so did his friends and the Samaritan army officers. "What does this bunch of poor, feeble Jews think they are doing?" he scoffed. "Do they think they can build the wall in a day if they offer enough sacrifices? And look at those charred stones they are pulling out of the rubbish and using again!"* (Nehemiah 4:1–2).

Not exactly esteem-building stuff, eh? If Nehemiah were looking for human approval, he would have given up already. Or at the very least, he would have been plagued with doubts. Instead he came up with an incredibly brilliant strategic response: "Then I prayed" (4:4).

Gee, who'd a thunk it?!?! Praying! The reality is, there will always be people who don't want to see you succeed, people who will actively try to thwart your efforts. Even people in the church! People who are supposed to be on the same team. It's useless to try to win them over and convince them you're right. The proper response to critics is prayer, because God is the only one who can do something about the situation. He's the only one who can change their hearts.

The minute you pray, the entire situation will turn around overnight! Then again, maybe it'll get worse:

> But when Sanballat and Tobiah and the Arabians, Ammonites, and Ashdodites heard that the work was going right ahead and that the breaks in the wall were being repaired, they became furious. They plotted to lead an army against Jerusalem to bring about riots and confusion. (4:7–8)

Has that ever happened to you? You pray to God and things actually get WORSE? Isn't that the pits? This is the very moment where you discover if you're operating on self-confidence or God-Confidence. If it's self-confidence, you'll be totally discouraged, angry at God and ready to give up. God-Confidence will enable you to press on: "But we prayed to our God and guarded the city day and night to protect ourselves" (4:9). They prayed . . . and they took action.

> "The work is so spread out," I explained to them, "and we are separated so widely from each other, that when you hear the trumpet blow you must rush to where I am; and God will fight for us" (4:19).

There's God-Confidence in Technicolor for you. They'll do the rushing, but GOD will do the fighting. God-Confidence doesn't mean that if you want a peanut butter and jelly sandwich, you sit in your bedroom confident God will make you one and bring it upstairs. It means you eat something nutritious, but GOD nourishes it to your body. It means you do what you can, but trust God with the results. (By the way, for best results, the peanut butter should be pure, unprocessed, with no salt added, the jelly should be 100 percent all-fruit, and the bread should be homemade whole-wheat. Just thought I'd throw that little nutritional advice in, no extra charge!)

Eventually, Sanballat sends a threatening letter to Nehemiah and concludes by saying, "I suggest that you come and talk it over with me—for that is the only way you can save yourself!" (Nehemiah 6:7).

Since Nehemiah had no intention of saving himself, he didn't bother to go to the meeting that, by the way, was to be held in the Valley of Ohno. If anyone invites you to meet with them in a place called "Oh No!" you ought to stay home, too. If Nehemiah had tried to save himself, he would have robbed God of the opportunity to do the saving. He would have stolen God's glory. Fortunately, he let God do the rescuing. God *did* rescue and as a result, he was glorified:

> *When our enemies and the surrounding nations heard about it, they were frightened and humiliated, and they realized that the work had been done with the help of our God.* (6:16)

I think we can glean five principles for escaping the Approval Trap:

Principle #1. Just because you're serving God with the best of intentions doesn't mean everyone will approve. In fact, there's almost always a critic.

Principle #2. Don't respond to your critics. Pray, and let God handle the rest.

Principle #3. Sometimes when we pray, the situation actually gets worse. Don't let that shake your confidence!

Principle #4. Take action, but put your confidence in God for the results.

Principle #5. Don't try to save yourself. Let God do the rescuing and he'll receive the glory.

Take Time to Reflect

1. Do you tend to think that since you're serving God with good intentions, everyone will approve and things will flow smoothly? Is that ever really the case?

2. Is there a critic (or group of critics) who seem intent on thwarting what God is calling you to accomplish? Resolve *not* to respond directly to your critics! Instead, write out a prayer to *God* and let him handle the rest.

3. Have you ever prayed . . . and the situation actually got worse? Describe what happened and how you responded.

4. What key lesson did you glean from today's study?

Confidence Boosters:

- Sometimes when we pray, the situation actually gets worse! Don't let that shake your confidence!
- Don't respond to your critics. Pray, and let God handle the rest.
- Don't try to save yourself. Let God do the rescuing and he'll receive the glory.

Day Four

Set Free From the Comparison Trap

Let everyone be sure that he is doing his very best, for then he will have the personal satisfaction of work well done and won't need to compare himself with someone else. Each of us must bear some faults and burdens of his own. For none of us is perfect!

Galatians 6:4–5

"I don't know why they pay you to speak," my daughter Nikki remarked one day. "All you do is tell stories about ME!" I must admit, I do like telling stories about my kids. And today I've got a real winner for you, even though it's not about winning.

When Nikki was in seventh grade, she qualified to compete in the 100-meter race at her junior high school's annual track competition. She spent weeks preparing herself physically and emotionally for the event. When the big day finally arrived, I sat down with her at the breakfast table.

"Nikki, I don't remember a whole lot about my track days," I confessed, "but I can tell you this much: if you want to win the race, don't look at the other runners. They'll only distract you. Focus on your own race and keep your eyes on the finish line. You got it?"

"Yeah, I got it," she assured me. "I'm not gonna look at the other runners. I'm gonna keep my eyes on that finish line and run my own race."

Amazing! With my superior parenting skills, I had actually communicated effectively with a teenager! Feeling very pleased that my pep talk had gotten through, I said, "Okay then! I'll see you at the track!"

Well, I arrived at the track meet with flowers in hand, ready to cheer Nikki on to victory. Unfortunately, when the gun went off, her head went *left*. I'm telling you, that girl ran the entire race with her head to the side. And you know what? She finished dead last. But you want to know the real irony? I wrote down the winning times in all three heats of the race. In every case, the winning time was 14 seconds or more. In a previous race, Nikki had been clocked at 13.9 seconds. She was capable of running faster than every girl who won out on the track that day. So why did she finish in last place? She looked at the other runners! That is, she fell into the Comparison Trap.

If we're not careful, the Comparison Trap will trip us up, too. Have you noticed that women are constantly comparing themselves with one another? It's like a national obsession! We compare our hair, our clothes, our bodies. (I'm still looking for someone whose thighs are more disproportionate to the rest of their body than mine. Feel free to send photographs for my consideration.) We compare our husbands and our kids. We compare our status as working or stay-at-home moms. We're constantly comparing! And what good ever comes of it? None!

I want to take apart today's verse, bit by bit, substituting her for him:

"Let everyone be sure . . ." Yes, we need to be sure. We need to examine ourselves to ensure that we are indeed "running with perseverance the race marked out for us."

". . . that she is doing her very best." HER very best. Not the very best that's ever been done in the history of human civilization. Not the best conceivable. Not even the best she *could do* if it weren't for her preschool children or her battle with arthritis and hot flashes. No, her very best given the circumstances she finds herself in.

" . . . for then she will have the personal satisfaction of work well done . . ." Notice that it doesn't say everyone's satisfaction. As we've already discussed, there will always be critics. There will always be someone who knows how you should have done it differently or how you could have done it better. That's their problem, not yours. Do you know in your heart that you did the best you could do? Okay, be satisfied then.

" . . . and won't need to compare herself with someone else." Here's the key: you won't *need* to compare yourself. When you live your life before God alone, when you let him be your judge, then it really

doesn't matter what anyone else does or says. You know where you stand with God.

"Each of us must bear some faults and burdens of her own. For none of us is perfect!" That's why it's never fair to compare your insides to someone else's outsides. You have no idea what's happening in their lives, and they don't know what's happening in yours, either. They may be living magnificently well, given their background, abilities, and current obstacles, even though you think their life is in shambles. And the woman who appears to have it all together may simply be fooling everyone but God.

Of course, it's easy for me to sit here and write about all these profound spiritual insights. But can I let you in on a little secret? I am TERRIBLE with this! I am constantly looking at the other runners. Here's how my Comparison Trap works: Whenever I get a book by another female Christian author, I immediately look in the front of the book to see if it lists her birth date. Then I quickly calculate to see if she is ahead of me in the race to write the most profound Christian book at the youngest possible age. I mean, you can see that this is a race, can you not?

If she appears to be ahead of me, I decide right then and there: I don't like her. I begin to wonder if *GOD* even likes her.

This is actually true.

Pretty pathetic, huh?

Anyway, when I do that, I get frantic and neurotic and just plain *not nice* to be around. I get so focused on what someone else has or has not done, on how well her race seems to be going compared to mine, that I lose sight of what God wants me to do. I forget to run my own race.

Do yourself a favor: don't compare yourself. Don't let yourself get distracted by Susie or Barbara and how well her race seems to be going compared to yours. Instead, "fix your eyes on Jesus, the author and perfecter of your faith."

I'll try to do the same!

Take Time to Reflect

1. Examine your heart. Can you honestly say that you are doing your very best? If not, what changes do you need to make?

2. What are some of the limitations in your life that you need to take into consideration when you evaluate what your "very best" can be?

3. Is personal satisfaction enough for you? Or are you only satisfied when *everyone else* (or some specific someone) is satisfied? Again, what changes might you need to make in terms of your expectations?

4. Who do you tend to compare yourself to? How and why? Resolve to break free from comparing yourself to others!

5. What key lesson did you glean from today's study?

Confidence Boosters:

- Don't look at the other runners! They'll only distract you.
- Run your own race, fixing your eyes on Jesus, the author and perfecter of your faith.

Day Five

Set Free From the Bitterness Trap

Have you ever noticed how one trap can lead to another? I sure have! I once read a poem that shook me to the core. There was one line in particular I've never been able to forget. It said, "A bitter old person is one of the crowning works of the devil." As I examined my heart, I knew that there were many areas where bitter roots were beginning to take hold. I realized that my life could not glorify God until I had been set free from the Bitterness Trap.

The Old Testament paints a tragic portrait of a bitter old person who became one of the crowning works of the devil. His name was Saul. Let's examine his life to glean lessons on how we can avoid the Bitterness Trap:

> But something had happened when the victorious Israeli army was returning home after David had killed Goliath. Women came out from all the towns along the way to celebrate and to cheer for King Saul, and were singing and dancing for joy with tambourines and cymbals. However, this was their song: "Saul has slain his thousands, and David his ten thousands!" Of course Saul was very angry. "What's this?" he said to himself. "They credit David with ten thousands and me with only thousands. Next they'll be making him their king!" So from that time on King Saul kept a jealous watch on David. (1 Samuel 18:6–9)

Saul just took the first step toward becoming one of Satan's crowning works, but notice it doesn't start with bitterness. Where does it start? The Comparison Trap. It's not enough that people were singing for joy, applauding Saul's accomplishments. It wasn't enough that God had enabled him to be part of a tremendous victory. He *compared* himself to David, rather than rejoicing that God had raised

107

up a warrior under the King's command. After the comparison came the jealousy.

Of course, the Comparison Trap inevitably leads to jealousy or pride. We either come up short or consider ourselves superior. Either way, it's a setup. The sorry saga continues:

> *The very next day, in fact, a tormenting spirit from God over-whelmed Saul, and he began to rave like a madman. David began to soothe him by playing the harp, as he did whenever this happened. But Saul, who was fiddling with his spear, suddenly hurled it at David, intending to pin him to the wall. But David jumped aside and escaped. This happened another time, too, for Saul was afraid of him and jealous because the Lord had left him and was now with David. Finally Saul banned him from his presence and demoted him to the rank of captain. But the controversy put David more than ever in the public eye. David continued to succeed in everything he undertook, for the Lord was with him.* (18:10–14)

I'm not brave enough to touch that line about "a tormenting spirit from God." If you're part of a weekly Bible study, ask your leader to explain it. (Shameless, huh?) However, one thing in the passage is clear: God's favor rested upon David and no matter how outraged and outrageous Saul became, no matter how many dirty tricks he tried to pull, nothing could stop what God had ordained. All of Saul's attempts to "dethrone" David were in vain. In fact, every time he tried to pull David down, God lifted David higher.

Just between the two of us, have you ever tried to tear somebody down? Be completely honest. Someone you were jealous of: at school, in the workplace, maybe even at your church. And no matter how hard you tried to "cut her down to size," her star just kept rising. Didn't it make you crazy?

I'm ashamed to admit this, but I've played the game, too. Sometimes when I see a dynamic Christian author or speaker whom God is using in a mighty way, rather than rejoicing that the kingdom is advancing, I'm overcome with jealousy. Sometimes the jealousy goes a step further and I look for little opportunities to "cut her down to size." It's always a losing battle.

I've been on the other side of the game, too. I've been the one someone else was determined to "take down a notch or two." Just my luck, she happened to be very good at "taking down" and wouldn't settle for anything less than twenty notches! It's painful and downright frightening. Has it ever happened to you? Maybe, right now, there is someone who is determined to "dethrone" you—determined to thwart what God is doing in your life and ministry. Be encouraged. The lives of David and Saul provide clear evidence that no human being—not even the king—can bring you down when God intends to lift you up. You might be interested in studying David's response to Saul's attacks. He refused to take matters into his own hands, instead entrusting his future to the One who judges justly. That's what Total God-Confidence is all about.

Unfortunately, Saul was unwilling to admit the obvious. Rather than repenting and getting on board with God's agenda, he allowed hate to consume his mind while bitterness destroyed his heart:

> *When the king realized how much the Lord was with David and how immensely popular he was with all the people, he became even more afraid of him, and grew to hate him more with every passing day.* (1 Samuel 18:28–29)

Saul was chosen by God. He was called into ministry. He was given incredible opportunities and glorious victories. He was the Golden Boy for a season, but it all ended in ruin. What a humbling lesson to us all.

Ministry is a privilege, but there are potential pitfalls. I believe the Bitterness Trap (which almost always begins with the Comparison and/or the Approval Trap) is chief among them. As one who is in ministry and, yes, one who is prone to bitterness, I've given much thought to these issues.

After considerable time spent in prayer, I've developed two sure-fire strategies to avoid the Bitterness Trap.

The first is the one we've talked about all week: *Serve for the glory of God alone. Don't look for human approval and don't compare yourself to anyone else.* Try it. It works.

Now here's the second strategy: *Give up ministry entirely and devote yourself instead to eating bonbons and watching game shows.*

What do you think? Hey, it is *not* a dumb idea. It will work! Follow my logic here. If you devote yourself to bonbons and game shows, when you come to the end of your life, you'll be a mediocre Christian.

But at least you won't be a *bitter* Christian.

Better to be mediocre than bitter. Think about it.

Then ask God to give you the grace to choose strategy #1.

Take Time to Reflect

1. What lessons did you learn from the lives of Saul and David?

2. Is there someone you've tried to "dethrone?" Write out a prayer of confession and repentance. Ask him to cleanse you. Make amends if necessary.

3. Is there someone who is actively trying to "dethrone" you? Don't let them shake you; instead, walk in Total God-Confidence.

4. Are you on the road to becoming: a mediocre Christian, a bitter Christian, or a Christian who walks in Total God-Confidence?

5. What key lesson did you glean from today's study?

6. Write out This Week's Verse from memory.

Confidence Boosters:

- A bitter old person is one of the crowning works of the devil.
- Better to be a mediocre Christian than a bitter one.

Weekly Review:

See if you can fill in the ten characteristics of walking in Total God-Confidence. Look in the back of the book if you need help:

C _____ according to his purpose

O _____ to his plan

N _____ by his love

F _____ from the chains that bind

I _____ conformed to his character

D _____ in his Word

E _____ by faith

N _____ shaken by the jerks

C _____ that he is able and faithful

E _____ to take the leap of faith

WEEK FIVE:

Increasingly Conformed to His Character

This Week's Verse:

For this very reason, make every effort to add to your faith
goodness; and to goodness, knowledge; and to knowledge, self-
control; and to self-control, perseverance; and to perseverance,
godliness; and to godliness, brotherly kindness; and to brotherly
kindness, love. For if you possess these qualities in increasing
measure, they will keep you from being ineffective and
unproductive in your knowledge of our Lord Jesus Christ.

2 Peter 1:5–8 (NIV)

Day One

Getting Away With Something

Do not be deceived: God cannot be mocked. A man reaps what he sows.   Galatians 6:7 NIV

Recently the city of Phoenix (the major city near my home) came up with a new technological advance that I am not happy about. It's called photoradar.[1]

Have you heard of this? If not, I'll enlighten you, but first I want you to examine your conscience and answer a very important question: Do you consider speed limits more of a suggestion? You know, sort of a starting point. So if it says 50 mph, it's more like 50ish. I'll admit, that's always been my philosophy. Hey, as long as I didn't get caught, I figured I was "getting away with something."

Well, here's how this horrible photoradar works. You wake up one morning, perfectly innocent, and you realize you're late for an appointment. So you hop in the car and start driving like a maniac. You're digging through your purse and pulling out makeup. You've got one eye on the road while you look in the rearview mirror to put on your base and your blush and your lipstick. Then comes the ultimate test: putting on mascara while you drive, just praying you don't hit a pothole. I mean, you have places to go, things to do, people to see! You don't have time to get bogged down with little details like obeying the speed limit. *(Please tell me I'm not the only woman who does this!)*

You make it to your destination—only about five minutes late, which is actually early in my book—and it looks like you got away with it. You return home, and all is well in the universe. But lo and behold, several weeks later a *ticket* arrives in the mail.

---

[1] I'm indebted to my former pastor, Bob Fox, of Red Mountain Community Church, for the photoradar illustration.

Photoradar gotcha!

You see, these photoradar devices capture your speed limit and photograph your license plate. Then it goes into a computer, they check the registration, find out your name and address, and mail you the speeding ticket. There's no chance to cry and talk them out of it. (*What? You don't do that, either?*)

You thought you had gotten away with something, but you really didn't. You did what seemed expedient at the time, and you had no idea what it cost you—*until the ticket came due.*

You know, I may chuckle and say, "Well, breaking the speed limit is no big deal. It's not like I *murdered* someone on the freeway. I just broke the speed limit." But the Bible says that we are to submit to those in authority. So if those in authority set the limit at 45 mph, that's the speed we should go. It may seem like a small thing, but life is made up of small things that add up over time.

As I thought about photoradar, I realized how powerfully it illustrated much of my life. God began to deal with me in so many areas. Always in a big hurry. Running here and there, trying to get where I wanted to go, trying to make it to my destination according to my timetable—disregarding the rules of the game of life. Doing what seemed expedient at the time. Thinking I was "getting away with something," and having no idea what it had cost me—*until the ticket came due.*

When I was a young woman in high school, I disdained the girls who took home economics courses. I was never going to get married and have children. BORING! I was in a big hurry to get to college. I was gonna make it to the Ivy League, and I didn't care what it took to get there. So I never learned the fine art of homemaking. I never learned to cook or sew or decorate my home or make holidays special or care for a husband and children. I didn't even learn how to clean my room or do my laundry. My mom did all that because, after all, I was too busy. I had places to go, things to do, people to see! I did not have time for such small stuff. Besides, I thought I was getting away with something.

But you know, one day I grew up, moved out of my parents' house, and had no clue how to run a household. If any of you ever come look at my house or taste my cooking, you'll know I haven't been able to make up for that lost time. I did what seemed expedient, and I never knew what it cost me—*until the ticket came due.*

Then it was off to college, and then corporate America. I climbed aboard the corporate express and started traveling at breakneck speed. I was in a hurry to go as far and as fast as I could. I worked 50, 60, 70 hours per week, and eventually I was moderately successful. Did I mention that I had gotten married along the way? Not to worry, I did not let that distract me from my destination. After all, I had places to go, things to do, people to see! Then I woke up one night and looked at the man in bed next to me. I realized he was a total stranger. I thought I was getting away with something. I did what seemed expedient at the time, and I never knew what it cost me—*until the ticket came due.*

My husband and I bought a house and we set to work fixing the place up and furnishing it. We noticed the empty room at the end of the hall and we thought, *Someday we'll have a baby, and that will be the nursery.* Meanwhile, we were on the run. We had places to go, things to do, people to see! We did not have time to settle down and start a family. Then I looked in the mirror one day and said, "Donna, you're almost thirty years old. This business of having a baby is not quite as simple as you thought it was going to be."

Now I'm closing in on forty, and wishing I had started building my family a lot earlier. I was too busy to take time for little ones. I did what seemed expedient at the time, and I never knew what it cost me—*until the ticket came due.*

When we finally had our first child after eight years of marriage, I felt strongly that God would have me stay home with my baby. But since we had maxed out our credit cards, we needed a second income just to make the monthly payments. I decided to launch a home business. On more days than I care to admit, all my daughter Leah ever heard from me was "Not now, Mommy's busy." I did not have time for small stuff like playing dolls or skipping rope or coloring. I didn't have time to pay attention to my child; I was too busy running a home business so I could . . . why was I doing that? Oh yeah, I forgot. I was running a home business so I could stay home with my child. What's wrong with this picture?

All those days I ignored her so I could get something accomplished, I thought I was getting away with something. I was wrong.

Seven years later, I finally gave birth to another child. So often

I'll say to Leah, "Honey, why don't you go play with your baby sister?" And she says, in essence, "Not now, Leah's busy." It breaks my heart. I thought I was getting away with something. I did what seemed expedient at the time, and I never knew what it cost me—*until the ticket came due.*

I don't know where you are today, but I suspect that in some area of your life, tickets are coming due. I've learned a very simple truth: There's no such thing as "getting away with something." The Bible assures us that this is quite impossible. "Do not be deceived: God cannot be mocked. A man reaps what he sows."

What's true in the practical realm is true in the spiritual realm, as well. We may think we're "getting away with something" when we skip our time with God, when we fail to devote time to the study of his Word. We may think we're "getting away with something" when we make the things of God the lowest priority in our lives. But God cannot be mocked. Sooner or later, the ticket will come due.

God's goal is that we would be increasingly conformed to his character, that we would become an increasingly accurate reflection of his glory. If we cooperate with him, if we slow down and attend to our spiritual lives, the process is beautiful. If we refuse to cooperate, then he has to deal with us the hard way.

Throughout this week, we'll be looking at the ways—both the joyful and the painful—in which God conforms us to his character.

Take Time to Reflect

1. Are you a woman on the run? Write a prayer expressing your desire to slow down and cultivate the character of God in your life.

2. React to the photoradar illustration. Indicate areas in which you have tried to "get away with something."

3. Are there any tickets coming due in your life?

4. What key lesson did you glean from today's study?

5. Turn to the back of the book and remove your Bible verse card for this week.

Confidence Boosters:

- There's no such thing as "getting away with something."
- You can spend your life on the run, doing what seems expedient at the time, but sooner or later, the ticket comes due.

Day Two

Everything We Need

His divine power has given us everything we need for life and godliness through our knowledge of him who called us by his own glory and goodness. Through these he has given us his very great and precious promises, so that through them you may participate in the divine nature and escape the corruption in the world caused by evil desires. For this very reason, make every effort to add to your faith goodness; and to goodness, knowledge; and to knowledge, self-control; and to self-control, perseverance; and to perseverance, godliness; and to godliness, brotherly kindness; and to brotherly kindness, love. For if you possess these qualities in increasing measure, they will keep you from being ineffective and unproductive in your knowledge of our Lord Jesus Christ. 2 Peter 1:3–8 NIV

Quite a verse, isn't it? It's jam-packed with truth, which is why we're going to focus on it all week, tackling it bit-by-bit. First, I notice an amazing truth: "His divine power has given us *everything we need* for life and godliness" (emphasis added).

He has given it to us, handed it to us . . . but have we received it? Have we appropriated it? Are we availing ourselves of that power on a daily basis? The answer, in many cases, is no.

Many Christians' lives lack power. They assume it's because there is no power available; not so. God has *given us* everything we need to live godly lives. The power is there. No question about that. The only question is: will we tap into that power or not?

Let's assume you want a life of power. You want to grow in godliness. How is that accomplished? ". . . through our *knowledge* of him who called us" [emphasis added].

I am continually amazed when I talk with women at retreats and conferences by how many of their problems boil down to one simple problem: Their God is too small. Because they have a tiny, impotent God, they can't walk by faith. How can you have faith in a powerless, absentee God? The kind of God who was nice enough to send his Son two thousand years ago, but has since been far too preoccupied to involve himself in the lives of his children?

It is our KNOWLEDGE of him that provides access to the power through which we can lead godly lives. The problem with many of us, dare I say most of us, is simple: We don't really know our God. We don't know his character.

Fortunately, there are a number of ways to rectify this problem. Some simple; some complex. Some can be tackled in a few weeks; some will require a lifetime. Let me suggest three steps:

1. Complete the Kay Arthur study *Lord, I Want to Know You*, which explores many of the names of God recorded in the Bible. Since God's names reflect his character and attributes, the more you understand his names, the better you will know your God. You can do this study with a group or individually. I have completed the study twice and found it both eye-opening and life-changing.

2. Read and study your Bible daily. (Novel idea, eh?) Don't bring preconceived ideas to the text. Watch God in action and let those actions speak for themselves.

3. Cultivate your personal walk with God. This, of course, is a lifelong journey. To speed you along, I would recommend *Experiencing God* by Henry Blackaby, and my devotional book *Becoming a Vessel God Can Use*.

Now I have to preface the rest of today's comments with a warning: We're about to head into dangerous doctrinal territory. I'm even going to reveal my latent Calvinist sympathies! You can feel free to disagree with me, and I'll still love you. (Gee, I hope you'll still love me?!?!) But please, at least think about what I'm saying and ponder the implications.

I believe this verse tells us something vitally important about our God: "who *called us* by his own glory and goodness" (emphasis added).

Our God is an active, initiating God. He is the one who seeks a relationship with us. Indeed, I believe he yearns for a relationship with us with far more passion than we yearn for him. It is he who *called us. He didn't wait for you to come to him; he went looking for you.*

Now I don't want to get into a huge debate about predestination and election. This isn't the time or place, but I can't resist throwing this out for your consideration: The word couplet "free will" does not appear anywhere in the Bible. There doesn't appear to be any indication of anyone choosing to follow God *until they were called by him.* In contrast, the word "chosen" appears 125 times (in the *New International Version* of the Bible). The word "called" appears 504 times. Just something to think about.

My point is this: We don't serve a wimpy, passive God who's sitting up in heaven, hoping people will like him, hoping people will choose to follow him, hoping believers will get to work impressing people so they'll want to become Christians. Unfortunately, wrong theology leads to wrong priorities. That's how we get prayer requests like "Dear God, please let my daughter become the Homecoming Queen so everyone will know how beautiful and popular Christians are. Then her whole high school will be won to Christ." Frankly, I think God's bigger than that. I think he knows exactly what he's doing on this planet and all of our efforts trying to "impress people into the kingdom" are fruitless.

God's desire is that we would participate in the divine nature and escape the corruption in the world. He wants us to be a holy people, set apart for his purposes. Incidentally, the word holy can also be rendered peculiar. If there's nothing in your life that your unbelieving neighbors consider peculiar, maybe you should spend less time trying to "win them" and more time "participating in the divine nature and escaping the corruption in the world."

Make every effort to know your God and to become the kind of person he has called you to be. He'll take care of the rest.

Take Time to Reflect

1. Is your God too small?

2. What steps do you need to take this week to begin tapping into the "divine power"?

3. What actions do you need to take to ensure that you are growing in "your knowledge of him"?

4. Is there any significance (or implications for your lifestyle) in the truth that "he called you by his own glory and goodness"?

5. Write out a prayer thanking God for calling you.

6. What key lesson did you glean from today's study?

Confidence Boosters:

- Ultimately, wrong theology leads to wrong priorities.
- We tap into divine power by growing in our knowledge of God.

Day Three

If You Possess These Qualities
in Increasing Measure . . .

Let's spend another day dealing with this megaverse.

> *His divine power has given us everything we need for life and godliness through our knowledge of him who called us by his own glory and goodness. Through these he has given us his very great and precious promises, so that through them you may participate in the divine nature and escape the corruption in the world caused by evil desires. For this very reason, make every effort to add to your faith goodness; and to goodness, knowledge; and to knowledge, self-control; and to self-control, perseverance; and to perseverance, godliness; and to godliness, brotherly kindness; and to brotherly kindness, love. For if you possess these qualities in increasing measure, they will keep you from being ineffective and unproductive in your knowledge of our Lord Jesus Christ.*   2 Peter 1:3–8 NIV

I notice it's loaded with lots of big words like perseverance, and unfathomable concepts like election. But do you know what the most important word in the passage is? Just a simple, itty-bitty two-letter word: if: "If you possess these qualities . . ."

"If" means there's a condition. It's not automatic. "If you possess these qualities . . ." Then what? "They will keep you from being ineffective and unproductive in your knowledge of Christ." Do you realize it's possible to be a Christian, to slip into heaven under the blood, yet your time here on earth would have been *ineffective and unproductive*? Isn't that sad? Isn't it tragic to think you could pass through this life completely missing the purpose for which God created you?

How would you characterize your life? Are you productive and effective? Here are the words that *ought to* describe you:

- faith
- goodness (or virtue)
- knowledge
- self-control (or temperance)
- perseverance
- godliness
- brotherly kindness
- love (or charity)

Do you have all these nailed down?

What? Not yet?

Now, before you start getting depressed on me, I also have a word of encouragement. Do you know what I love about the Bible? It's so realistic. What does it say? "If you possess these qualities in *increasing measure . . .*" (emphasis added). As long as you are making forward progress, that's what matters in God's sight. God knows we're imperfect. He knows no one is going to master these characteristics. Yet we should be seeking to grow in godliness.

This is one of the great paradoxes of the Christian life: God has given us everything we need . . . and we must make every effort to add to our faith. This paradox is seen even in the Old Testament: "You must obey all of my commandments, for I am the Lord who sanctifies you" (Leviticus 20:8).

It is God who makes us holy; but we must strive to be holy. We are saved by grace; but we must avail ourselves of the means of grace. His divine power has given us everything we need; yet we have to *make every effort to add to our faith.*

Our eternal salvation is not at issue here, assuming you have prayed through the "Steps to Freedom" (at the back of the book). What's at stake is the quality of our service to our King. Oh, sure, we can try to "get away with something" and live mediocre Christian lives, but we'll reap the consequences of our choices, forgiveness notwithstanding.

Let's resolve to forget trying to get away with something, devoting the bare minimum to our walk with God, and instead *make every effort* to become women characterized by virtue, self-control, and love.

Today's lesson is intentionally brief, because I want you to set aside time for serious self-evaluation. Ponder the characteristics that ought to describe a growing Christian. Are you being increasingly conformed to the character of Christ? Ask God to open your mind and heart to areas that need growth. Also try to visualize what your life would look like if you were to "make every effort." What would your schedule be like? What items would have to be added? What items would need to be eliminated?

God is calling you to "make every effort." Will you heed the call?

Take Time to Reflect

1. As you reflect upon your Christian life, do you feel it has been effective and productive? Why or why not? Are changes needed?

2. Do you make *every effort* . . . or do you barely make any effort to grow in your Christian life? (Maybe you're like me—somewhere in between!) Honestly evaluate where you are on the "effort scale" and note what changes you might need to make.

3. Look up Psalm 34:1–10 and note God's word of encouragement for you.

4. Write out a prayer, asking God to empower you to "make every effort."

5. What key lesson did you glean from today's study?

Confidence Boosters:

- It's possible to be a Christian yet be completely ineffective and unproductive in the kingdom of God.
- God supplies everything we need, but we have to make every effort.

Day Four

The Power of Companionship

I'd like you to think for a moment about the power of companionship. It is most obvious among children. Bobby gets a yo-yo, and all of his friends have to have one. Susie's best friend becomes obsessed with the latest music group, and before long Susie has a poster of the group on her bedroom wall. What's true among children is also true among adults, with perhaps more subtlety.

No matter how independent or unique we consider ourselves, the truth is, we become like the people we spend time with. I once heard it said that who you will be in five years depends largely on two factors: (1) the books you read and (2) the people you spend time with.

You may find that encouraging or frightening, depending on the books you're reading (you *don't* read those trashy romance novels, do you?) and the character of your friends (you *do* talk about something other than other people, right?).

If who you are is not who you hope to become, the surest remedy is improving the quality of the books you read and the people you spend time with. What better book to read than God's Word? Who better to spend time with than God himself?

Theoretically, if you will simply read God's Word and spend time with him, you will find that in five years you will be increasingly conformed to his character.

If it were that simple, though, we'd all act like saints.[1]

Let me ask you a question. Promise to answer truthfully, now! Do you ever fall asleep during prayer? Does your mind drift? I mean, did you ever think, *Okay, this is it. I'm going to spend an hour in prayer,* and about five minutes into the prayer time you ran out of things to say? And when you tried to listen for God, all you heard was your

---

[1] Positionally, in Christ, we ARE saints. But do we live like saints ought to live?

stomach rumbling? Or when you tried to picture the majesty of God's throne room, Mel Gibson floated into view?

Or is it just me. . . ?

Prayer is hard for many reasons. Obviously, the last thing the enemy of your soul wants is to hear you communing with God. Therefore, he'll do anything to distract you. But there's something more, something deeper. There's an inner bankruptcy. In our modern world, we've forgotten how to cultivate the inner life. As the world around us becomes increasingly complex, as the volume of existence cranks up, we find it harder and harder to simply sit and listen to the silence.

I used to flatter myself that I didn't pray because I didn't have time. I wish it were that simple. Then all I would have to do would be to clear my schedule (piece of cake, right?) and I'd be praying to the high heavens. The truth is, we don't know how to deal with solitude. When we look within our souls, we realize we're gazing into a deep, deep well. Unfortunately, for many of us, the well is empty. When we seek to draw refreshment, we find the well has run dry.

I would like nothing more, at this point, than to offer up some quick (or at least surefire) solution to this inner bankruptcy. That wouldn't be honest. If there's a simple solution, I haven't found it. I think each of us, in the privacy of our soul, has to wrestle with this. I think it's part of living in a fallen world, especially a pyrotechnic world. Nevertheless, we need to find ways to feed our souls, to cultivate the inner life. It will take us all of our lives.

In closing, let me make one suggestion, by way of personal example. In February 1997 I desperately needed to draw upon internal resources. Unfortunately, the well came up empty. So I picked up the phone and called the Franciscan Renewal Center (in Scottsdale, Arizona) on the off-chance that they might help me run away from home. As it turns out, they were delighted to accommodate me for a private retreat. I spent three days living among the monks in complete silence: no conversation, no phone, no radio, not even a clock. Silence.

I brought along my Bible, some great Christian books, paper and pen. I had no schedule. I slept when I was tired, even if it was in the middle of the day. If I awoke, even if it was in the middle of the night, I assumed God had awakened me so we could talk. I wandered through the desert. I sat quietly in the prayer chapel. At mealtimes, one of the monks would ring the mission bell. I would walk to the dining room and quietly have my meal. Then back to my nonexistent schedule. It was incredibly life-changing.

Incidentally, it was there, on February 22, 1997, that God gave me the vision (including the title) for this book.

I've since learned that there are monasteries, convents, and retreat centers all over the country that will gladly open their doors for private retreats. I would encourage you to investigate what is available in your area. As for me, I think I'm just about due to run away from home again!

Take Time to Reflect

1. What's the status of your internal spiritual resources? Are you bankrupt?

2. Do you need to run away from home?

3. Jot down some ideas for how, when, and where you might have a silent retreat of your own. Do some investigating into local possibilities.

4. Write out a prayer asking God to show you the status of your internal spiritual resources.

5. What key lesson did you glean from today's study?

Confidence Boosters:

- Who you will be in five years is largely determined by the books you read and the people you spend time with.
- In our modern world, we have forgotten how to cultivate the inner life.

Day Five

The Grand Canyon Within

I t's pretty rare that I come up with an insight into the Bible that I feel is truly original. I mean, hey, there's nothing new under the sun, right? Well, I think I've got one today. (If you've heard this analysis before, please don't write to me and burst my little bubble.)

Lots of people choose Bible names for their children, hoping that their child will be inspired to emulate the wonderful qualities of his or her namesake. I named my daughter Leah because I liked the sound of it. The biblical Leah always struck me as a rather pathetic figure; sort of the fifth wheel in Jacob and Rachel's otherwise romantic marriage. I'll tell you in a minute why I think God has another view of her. But first, let's take a look at what I call Leah's "Grand Canyon Within":

> *Now Laban had two daughters, Leah, the older, and her younger sister, Rachel. Leah had lovely eyes, but Rachel was shapely, and in every way a beauty. Well, Jacob was in love with Rachel. So he told her father, "I'll work for you seven years if you'll give me Rachel as my wife."*
>
> *"Agreed!" Laban replied. "I'd rather give her to you than to someone outside the family." So Jacob spent the next seven years working to pay for Rachel. But they seemed to him but a few days, he was so much in love.*
>
> *Finally the time came for him to marry her. "I have fulfilled my contract," Jacob said to Laban. "Now give me my wife, so that I can sleep with her."*
>
> *So Laban invited all the men of the settlement to celebrate with Jacob at a big party. Afterwards, that night, when it was dark, Laban took Leah to Jacob, and he slept with her. (And Laban gave to Leah a servant girl, Zilpah, to be her maid.) But in the morning—it was Leah! "What sort of trick is this?" Jacob raged at Laban.*

"I worked for seven years for Rachel. What do you mean by this trickery?"

"It's not our custom to marry off a younger daughter ahead of her sister," Laban replied smoothly. "Wait until the bridal week is over and you can have Rachel too—if you promise to work for me another seven years!"

So Jacob agreed to work seven more years. Then Laban gave him Rachel, too. And Laban gave to Rachel a servant girl, Bilhah, to be her maid.

So Jacob slept with Rachel, too, and he loved her more than Leah, and stayed and worked the additional seven years.

But because Jacob was slighting Leah, Jehovah let her have a child, while Rachel was barren. So Leah became pregnant and had a son, Reuben (meaning "God has noticed my trouble"), for she said, "Jehovah has noticed my trouble—now my husband will love me."

She soon became pregnant again and had another son and named him Simeon (meaning "Jehovah heard"), for she said, "Jehovah heard that I was unloved, and so he has given me another son."

Again she became pregnant and had a son, and named him Levi (meaning "Attachment") for she said, "Surely now my husband will feel affection for me, since I have given him three sons!"

Once again she was pregnant and had a son and named him Judah (meaning "Praise"), for she said, "Now I will praise Jehovah!" (Genesis 29:16–35 TLB)

Leah claimed that if only she could have a son, she would be content. Guess what? God was faithful. He sent her four sons, but she wasn't content. She played the game of giving her servant girl to Jacob, so she could vicariously have more sons. Then she stooped as low as you can go. She hired her husband like a gigolo:

That evening as Jacob was coming home from the fields, Leah went out to meet him. "You must sleep with me tonight!" she said; "for I am hiring you with some mandrakes my son has found!" So he did. And God answered her prayers and she became pregnant again, and gave birth to her fifth son. She named him Issachar (meaning "Wages"), for she said, "God has repaid me for giving my slave-girl to my husband." Then once again she became pregnant, with a sixth son. She named him Zebulun (meaning "Gifts"), for she said, "God has given me good gifts for my husband. Now he will honor me, for I have given him six sons" (Genesis 30:16–20).

So now she has five sons, not counting the children her servant bore. Do you think she's content now? I doubt it. What's interesting to me, however, is not only that she's discontented after God gave her what she claimed she wanted, what she thought would fulfill her. There's something more here. Watch this:

> *A record of the genealogy of Jesus Christ, the son of David, the son of Abraham:*
> *Abraham was the father of Isaac,*
> *Isaac the father of Jacob,*
> *Jacob the father of Judah and his brothers,*
> *Judah. . . . (Matthew 1:1–3 NIV)*

We don't need to go any further than that. Judah was part of the line of David. Leah was one of the grandmothers of Jesus! With the birth of Judah, *she had fulfilled God's primary purpose for her life.* I didn't say it was her only purpose. Nor am I saying that women have no other function other than giving birth. My point is: We like to tell ourselves that if God would give us some profound assignment, if only we had a sense of purpose, then we'd be content with our lives. Yet Leah had accomplished what God had in mind for her, but she didn't even recognize it. She had a houseful of children—the very thing she prayed for—but it was never enough to fill the emptiness within her.

I think, more than anything else, she was looking for her husband's approval. God had set his approval upon her. He had answered her prayers and chosen her for the highest privilege anyone can have. Unfortunately, God's approval wasn't enough for her.

Some of us are like Leah. We have a hole in our heart the size of the Grand Canyon, so we hand our husband a bucket and say, "Here, you fill it." Or we hand it to our church, our friends, or what have you. We fail to realize that filling that hole is something only God can do. And he can only do it if we will let him.

Don't get me wrong. I think it would be nice if your husband met your needs. It would be nice if your church met your needs. It would be nice if your kids would get with the program. But if God is to us all he wants to be; if he is our all in all; if he is meeting all of your needs according to his riches in glory, then it's really not necessary.

As long as we think we'll be happy when we have "God AND _____," we'll never be able to glorify God. We'll never be able to give an accurate reflection of who he is. How can the world see God's reflection in a mud puddle? Our lives need to be so filled with God, so filled with that Living Water, that we show forth a brilliant reflection of his glory.

The message God has been speaking to my heart over the past year has been simply this: "I'm enough for you, Donna. Let me be enough." You don't need God plus financial security. You don't need God plus a great marriage. You don't need God plus anything. God is enough. Will you let him be to you all he wants to be? If you answer yes, he offers you a promise:

> *God is able to make it up to you by giving you everything you need and more, so that there will not only be enough for your own needs, but plenty left over to give joyfully to others.* (2 Corinthians 9:8)

When you allow God to meet your needs, you won't need a mere human to try to meet them. Then, rather than dealing with others out of your neediness, you can deal with them from a place of abundance. As you pour forth out of the abundance God gives, he will be glorified and you will be fulfilling the very purpose for which you were created.

Take Time to Reflect

1. To whom are you looking to meet your needs?

2. What effect has that "neediness" had on your relationship?

3. What practical steps can you take to begin looking to God to meet your needs, so that you can turn to others from a place of abundance?

4. Write out a prayer asking God to fill all your needs.

5. What key lesson did you glean from today's study?

6. Write out This Week's Verse from memory.

Confidence Boosters:

- Some of us have a hole in our heart the size of the Grand Canyon.
- Filling that hole is something only God can do.
- When God himself is meeting all of our needs, we can minister to others out of the abundance he gives.

Weekly Review:

See if you can fill in the ten characteristics of walking in Total God-Confidence. Look in the back of the book if you need help.

C_____ according to his purpose

O_____ to his plan

N_____ by his love

F_____ from the chains that bind

I _____ conformed to his character

D_____ in his Word

E_____ by faith

N_____ shaken by the jerks

C_____ that he is able and faithful

E_____ to take the leap of faith

WEEK SIX:
Daily
in His Word

This Week's Verse:

I will walk in my house with blameless heart. I will set before
my eyes no vile thing.

Psalm 101:2–3 (NIV)

Day One

Rich Man, Beggar Man

*So now we are slaves here in the land of plenty which you gave
to our ancestors! Slaves among all this abundance!*

Nehemiah 9:36

When I read this verse, it was like getting hit by a lightning bolt.
"Slaves among all this abundance!" Wow, does that sum up the
church in America, or what? Never has the body of Christ been so
blessed: churches on every corner, to suit every taste: quiet churches,
loud churches, small churches, big churches. Calvinists, dispensa-
tionalists, and whatever-works-for-you-ists. There's premillennial,
postmillennial, and a-millennial. Three services on Sunday morning
and one on Saturday night. You name it, you got it. We're talking one-
stop shopping. And speaking of one-stop shopping: Christian book-
stores; Christian book clubs; Christian videos; Christian audios;
Christian radio shows; Christian conferences for women, for men,
for couples, for singles.

There are an abundance of opportunities for us to "grow in the
grace and knowledge of our Lord Jesus Christ." But do we avail ourselves of these opportunities? Do we truly grab hold of the truths we
hear, let them seep deep down into our hearts and transform the way
we live? For the most part, the answer is no. Instead, most of us live
like slaves among abundance. We're still in bondage; slaves to sin.
Knowing what we ought to do, but too spiritually wimpy to bother to
do it.

It reminds me of a dream a friend of mine once had. In it, she
saw a blind old beggar walking along a crowded city street. She noticed that he was carrying two large shopping bags, and she assumed
they were filled with his meager possessions. Her heart was filled

with compassion as she watched him hobble along.

She approached the blind man and invited him to join her for a cup of coffee. He did, and as time passed he related his tale of woe. She learned about his life on the mean streets and the struggle to survive. When at last she had gained his confidence, she asked, "Sir, do you mind my asking what's in the bags?"

He looked puzzled. "I don't rightly know, Miss. But you're welcome to take a look."

When she opened the bags, she discovered that they were filled with thousands and thousands of dollars. He was rich, but he didn't even know it. He was rich, yet he wandered the streets begging bread.

You know, so often we're just like that blind man. God has given us everything we need. We have every reason to approach life with complete confidence, trusting God day by day to fill us with every good gift from his vast store of riches. Yet so often we wander the streets, begging bread.

We have the answers, sisters. They are all to be found in God's Word. And the power to live according to that Word is found in a personal, one-on-one relationship with the living God.

Take Time to Reflect

1. In what ways are you living like a "slave amid abundance"?

2. How are you like the blind man who didn't even recognize the riches he held in his hands?

3. Look up 2 Peter 1:3–4 and note God's word of encouragement.

4. Write out a prayer, asking God to open your eyes.

5. What key lesson did you glean from today's study?

6. Turn to the back of the book and remove your Bible verse card for this week.

Confidence Boosters:

- It's possible to be free in Christ, yet live like "slaves among all this abundance."
- In Christ, we have all the riches we could possibly need, if we would just grab hold of them.

Day Two

People Magazine

> *I will walk in my house with blameless heart. I will set before my eyes no vile thing.*   Psalm 101:2–3

My life is weird. I went from not being allowed to walk around the block unsupervised to becoming a pseudo-jet-setter, traveling to women's retreats around the country. Most flights begin and end uneventfully—thank heaven! But there's one I'll never forget. I was in an aisle seat on the left side, toward the back of the plane. I glanced across the aisle and there, in the middle seat, was a young woman who, immediately after settling in and buckling up, set a Bible on her tray. This was no ordinary Bible. It was a great-looking study Bible.

I smiled approvingly to myself.

A few moments later, she reached into her carry-on bag and pulled out *People* magazine. She carefully placed it on top of her Bible and proceeded to read it throughout the entire flight.

What a disgrace, I thought to myself. *A study Bible and no desire to study it. Tsk. Tsk.* It was a very smug moment. Then suddenly I heard a voice from heaven inquire, *"Uh, Donna. So where exactly is your Bible?"*

He had me.

You see, we may not be that blatant about it. We may not take out *People* magazine and deliberately put it on top of our Bibles. Nevertheless, that's exactly what we do every day. Every time you read a magazine, a novel, an interoffice memorandum, an e-mail, or a cereal box. Every time you gaze into the TV screen rather than gazing into God's Word, you're saying the same thing. You're saying, "What *People* has to say means more to me than what God has to say."

Think about it.

Then do something about it.

Sitting there on that plane, I made a resolution that led to a revolution. I resolved, first and foremost, never to read anything on an airplane other than my Bible. (I mean, gee, what if you see ME reading *People* magazine after you've read this diatribe. Not good!) That resolution alone got me through most of the New Testament.

I also resolved not to set anything before my eyes before I had looked into God's Word each day. I haven't been entirely faithful, but I've made great progress. Here's a helpful technique I have devised: Link whatever you read first to Bible reading. For example, I used to work on the Internet as a SYSOP. (That's a System Operator. Boy, talk about weird experiences! Anyway. . . .) So, I linked my Internet log-on with Bible reading. Each day I'd sit down at my computer, type in my password, and while waiting for the system to connect, I read my Bible.

Perhaps the first thing you read is the morning paper. Or the first thing you watch is *Good Morning, America*. Make the link. Make the resolution: "Before I can do X, I will read my Bible." Before you pick up the newspaper, pick up your Bible. Before you turn on the TV, pick up your Bible. The key to this algebraic equation is for X to be a constant, won't-miss item in your life.

My personal revolution became a family revolution in February 1998, when I bought the Bible Explorer software program for $15. (You can order one from my good friend Marita Littauer at 1–800–433–6633.) I discovered this nifty feature, the "Bible Reading Program," which tells you which chapters you have to read each day to complete the Bible in a year. More importantly, one click of a button will take you to that passage. Best of all, there's a "summary" feature, which will tell you, again with a simple click of a button, exactly what percentage of the Bible you have completed.

This was too cool. Each day, before using anything else on my computer, I'd load the Bible Explorer, click on the date, and it would transport me to the day's reading assignment. I'd click it again when finished reading, then click to see what percentage of the Bible I had completed.

Then I introduced my teenager, Nikki, to the exciting world of Bible Explorer. She got into it with a vengeance! One day I walked by her in the kitchen and casually mentioned that I had completed

35 percent of the Bible. She turned around and said, "Is that all? I'm at 37 percent."

At that moment, I did what any normal mother would do: I ran to my computer and read to 38 percent. When I tucked her into bed that night, I smiled and simply said: 38. She knew *exactly* what I meant. (Sometimes I can't believe I *didn't* give birth to this child. She's exactly like me!)

The race was on.

For the next several months, the competition in our house was fierce. At one point my husband looked at me, very puzzled, and said, "Are you sure this is normal?" A friend of mine heard about the competition and said, "Of course, you're going to let your daughter win, aren't you?"

"Are you kidding? No way!" I replied, with all the maternal affection I could muster.

Even my eight-year-old daughter, Leah, got in on the action. Believe it or not, she actually read through three—count 'em—three children's Bibles over the course of six months.

I am writing this during the first week of August 1998. Nikki finished reading the entire Bible several weeks ago. It took her less than seven months to accomplish a feat that, if the truth were told, most *adult* Christians have never even seriously attempted. Just this week, I bought Leah her fourth Bible. She told me today that Abraham must have loved God twice as much after what happened with Isaac. "Why is that?" I wondered. "Because then God gave him his son *twice*."

Wow.

As for me, I've completed 75 percent of the Bible and am determined to finish long before December 31![1]

I bet I can guess what you're thinking: *Yeah, yeah, yeah. That's just fine for Donna. She's a spiritual giant.* To which I respond, "Yeah, right. Where have you been throughout this entire book?"

Do you know what has been the most amazing lesson throughout this Bible revolution? Coming to grips with just how *incredibly easy* it is to read through the Bible in a year. To be honest, I used to feel very self-righteous when I would set the lofty goal of reading through

---

[1]Just an update for the truly curious: I finished the Bible in October.

the Bible in a year, as if Cecil B. DeMille himself would be impressed with this epic adventure.

There ain't nothin' to it, folks.

It's embarrassingly easy.

I am *not* organized. I am *not* a fast reader. I am *not* super-spiritual. And I don't have much free time. I'm just an ordinary homeschooling, homeworking mother of three (including a toddler) who sold one house, moved into another, traveled fifteen weekends out of the year, wrote this book, and *still* managed to read through most of the Bible without much effort.

If I can do it, anyone can. It's a simple matter of putting the first thing first. Will you make that resolution? If you do, get ready for a revolution!

P.S. Let me mention a few resources that have helped keep me motivated. My #1 secret weapon has been the audiocassette series *God's Masterwork: A Concerto in Sixty-Six Movements* by Chuck Swindoll. No one can bring the Bible to life like Pastor Swindoll does on this incredible five-volume set, featuring a sermon for virtually every book of the Bible. My approach has been to listen to the audiocassette as an introduction before tackling each book of the Bible. That way, I was excited about reading the book, plus I had a great overview of the key characters and themes I was about to encounter.

Each of the five volumes can be purchased separately. If you buy all five at once, it's gonna set you back about $228. If you can afford it, it's worth every penny. However, I realize that is pretty pricey for most folks. But you can do it the way I did: order the set one volume at a time. For example, I asked for Volume I (Genesis through 1 Chronicles) for my birthday. For Christmas, my daughter bought me Volume II, etc. (To order, contact Insight for Living at 1–800–772–8888 or check out their Web site: www.insight.org.)

The second resource is Henrietta Mears's magnum opus, *What the Bible Is All About* (published by Gospel Light). Although the book offers more detail than needed just to "get through" the Bible in a year, it's the perfect companion for when you're ready to tackle God's Word as a serious Bible student.

Next year, maybe?

Take Time to Reflect

1. When was the last time you read through the Bible in a year?

2. Will you resolve to read through the Bible in the next twelve months? What specific plans can you devise to help you achieve that goal?

3. What is the first thing you set before your eyes each day? Link that to your Bible reading and you'll be much more likely to stick with the program.

4. Look up Psalm 1 and note God's word of encouragement for you.

5. Write out a prayer expressing your commitment to give God's Word top priority in your life.

6. What key lesson did you glean from today's study?

Confidence Boosters:

- If you want to read the Bible faithfully, link the first thing you usually look at each morning with the Bible.
- Reading through the Bible in a year is embarrassingly easy!

Day Three

Do You Know Better Than She Does?

Not long ago, the First Christian Church of Any Town, U.S.A., was interviewing for a new Sunday school teacher. The leading candidate was a woman who had attended the church for forty-five years. The board of elders decided to keep the interview simple, so they asked the woman to recount her favorite Bible story. She thought for a moment, then announced that she'd like to retell the Parable of the Good Samaritan. Here's what she said,[1]

One day a man was traveling on the road from
Jericho to Jerusalem.
He fell down, and the thorns grew up and choked him.
He got up, but he didn't have any money.
Fortunately, he met the Queen of Sheba.
She gave him 1000 talents of gold and
1000 raiments of clothing.
Then he got in his chariot and drove furiously.
While he was driving, his hair got caught in a
Juniper Tree and he got hung up.
He hung there many days, but the Ravens
brought him food to eat and water to drink.
He ate 5,000 loaves of bread and two fish.
One night, while he was hanging there,
his wife, Delilah, came and cut off his hair.
And he fell on stony ground.
He got up and started to walk.
It began to rain.
And it rained for forty days and forty nights.
Finally, he came to the city and saw Queen Jezebel

---

[1]I'm indebted to Joshua Harris for this story.

sitting high in a castle window.
He said, "Throw her down." So they threw her down.
And he said, "Throw her down again."
So they threw her down 70 x 7.
Of the fragments that remained, they picked up
twelve baskets full, not including women and children.
Then they said, "Blessed are the peacemakers."
Now I just have one question for you Bible
scholars out there: "Whose wife will she be on that judgment
day?"

She sounds a little like some of us, doesn't she? We sorta know God's Word. I mean, we know it's in there somewhere, right? How can we walk in Total God-Confidence when we don't even know what God's Word SAYS? It's not enough to have little tidbits of knowledge and half-truths. If we're going to walk in Total God-Confidence, we've got to know what God's Word says.

Do you think you know your Bible better than our Sunday school teaching candidate? Okay then, go for it. I'm keeping this lesson intentionally brief, because I have a challenge for you. Today's assignment is to go through her rendition, line by line, and jot down where in the Bible you THINK the reference is taken from.

Only *after* you've recorded your guess, search your Bible and record the actual chapter and verse. (This will be too easy for those of you with Bible software. If you want a real challenge, use your old-fashioned Bible instead.)

I suspect this will prove an extremely humbling exercise for all of us.

Take Time to Reflect

1. Record your guesses.

2. Look up the actual passages and record the chapter and verse.

3. Repent in sackcloth and ashes!

4. What key lesson did you glean from today's study?

Confidence Boosters:

- It's not enough to know snippets and snatches of the Bible.
- We can't walk in Total God-Confidence unless we know exactly what God's Word says.

Day Four

Knowing God's Word by Heart

How can a young [woman] keep [her] way pure?
By living according to your word.
I seek you with all my heart;
do not let me stray from your commands.
I have hidden your word in my heart
that I might not sin against you.
I meditate on your precepts
and consider your ways.
I delight in your decrees;
I will not neglect your word.

Psalm 119:9–11, 15–16

I must admit, today's lesson is one that's "back by popular demand." For those of you who've already completed *Becoming a Vessel God Can Use*, this will be review.

If we want to walk in Total God-Confidence, we absolutely must know what God's Word says. That means not only a broad familiarity with the entire Bible, but an intimate knowledge of an increasing number of select passages.

I first began Scripture memory in earnest when I worked for the Billy Graham Crusade. The only way I could keep up with the large number of verses we had to memorize in counselor preparation was to carry them with me at all times. I wrote out each verse on a bunch of index cards and Post-it Notes. Everywhere I looked, there were Bible verses. They were in my coat, my purse, my pants pockets. I tucked them in my Bible, stuck them on shelves and on the kitchen counter. They were in the car, on my desk, and even under my pillow. My life looked like it had been invaded by an army of index cards.

It sounds crazy and it looks messy, but it works. You don't have to limit yourself to verses on evangelism, although that's a great place to start. Choose verses that address areas of need in your life or the life of your family.

When you know Scripture, you can have Total God-Confidence in the face of demonic attacks. When Satan tempted Jesus in the wilderness (Matthew 4:1–11), Jesus responded with confidence. He knew what God had said. Don't be duped like Eve, who fell for Satan's oldest line: "Did God really say. . . ?" (Genesis 3:1 NIV). Remember, Satan is the Father of Lies, and the only way to cut through his lies is with the truth. Jesus said, "Then you will know the truth, and the truth will set you free" (John 8:32 NIV). He also said, "I am the . . . truth" (John 14:6).

Know the truth and you can walk in Total God-Confidence.

Several years ago I was listening to a Chuck Swindoll sermon over the radio while driving in my car. The program was excellent, so I pulled over and jotted down his outline for Scripture memory. Guess where I wrote it? On an index card, of course! I still have that precious index card. Here's what I wrote:

Scripture Memory—
Memorize, Personalize, Analyze

1. Set aside fifteen minutes per day for Scripture memory.
2. Choose verses that address your weaknesses. That way, you'll have a vested interest in remembering them.
3. Read the passage aloud, over and over.
4. Break the verse down into logical parts. Learn one phrase, then two, until you've memorized the entire passage.
5. Repeat the reference often. (How many times have you searched for a verse in your Bible, murmuring that spaghetti sauce motto "It's in there"? If you can't find it, it's not much good. Learn the reference.)
6. It's better to learn a few verses really well, than many poorly.
7. Underline difficult terms or key words. Look them up in the dictionary, a concordance, or a Bible reference book.
8. Write out the verse from memory. This is a critical step. Something about putting pen to paper makes the words more permanent.

Thanks, Pastor Swindoll.

Here's a strategy I have used that sounds crazy—but I promise it works! It's so effective, I even got a letter from a missionary in Brazil who is using it. (She read the idea in *Becoming a Vessel God Can Use*.) I write out the first initial of every word in the verse, while looking at the passage. I set it down for a while. When I return, I try to complete the words from memory. Repeat this process several times and you'll be amazed to discover you remember that verse years later.

Another effective—and very painless—way to memorize Scripture is with Scripture songs. Many modern praise songs are Scripture set to music. As you sing along, God's Word is making its way into your heart. This year, during my read-through-the-Bible program, I couldn't help singing aloud when I got to familiar passages, especially throughout the Psalms.

Whatever method of Scripture memory you choose, the important thing is to spend time daily in his Word. Only then will you be able to walk in Total God-Confidence.

Take Time to Reflect

1. How can a woman keep her way pure?

2. What's the best way to face down temptation?

3. Can you think of a recent occasion when calling to mind a passage of Scripture might have helped?

4. Can you recall a recent occasion when you have seen the positive effect of memorizing God's Word? If you can't think of an example, what does that tell you?

5. Choose several verses you want to memorize. Transfer them onto index cards and/or Post-it Notes and get to work!

6. Write out a prayer expressing your commitment to Scripture memory.

7. What key lesson did you glean from today's study?

Confidence Boosters:

- When you memorize God's Word, you're better equipped to walk in Total-God Confidence.
- Repeatedly writing out a verse is one of the best ways to memorize Scripture.

Day Five

Checkpoints

When I was in high school, I ran on the cross-country team. Unlike ordinary track events, these competitions weren't held in comfortable arenas. Oh, no, no, no. Instead, each high school would map out the most challenging 3.5 miles they could possibly find. The more hills, rocks, streams, and fallen trees in the way, the better. Each school strived to have the most grueling cross-country course.

Two things stand out in my memory about my cross-country days. First, I finished dead last in every race. Well, except once, when this kid fell down and required stitches; I was able to step over him and finish second-to-last. Otherwise, it was a fairly inauspicious career, but it taught me a vital life lesson.

Throughout the course, there were checkpoints. At these checkpoints, a few things would happen. First, they'd jot down your number to make sure you had indeed made it up to that part of the race, that you weren't taking any shortcuts. Second, it was a reassurance to you, as the runner, that you were somehow, some way, making it through the wilderness. And third, it would be a time of refreshment. (They always served orange Gatorade!)

Let me ask you this: Have you established any CHECKPOINTS in your life? A checkpoint should serve three purposes, just like it did for my cross-country team:

1. *Accountability.* It should hold you accountable, to make sure you're not taking any shortcuts.
2. *Reassurance.* It should reassure you that you are, indeed, "running with perseverance the race marked out for you."
3. *Refreshment.* It should be a time to renew your spirit.

At the end of today's reading, you'll discover a tool for establishing checkpoints in your life. It's called the Weekly Evaluation Worksheet. Quite simply, it's designed to *force you* to stop once a week and reflect upon your life. What could be worse than coming to the end of your time on earth and discovering that you have missed the very purposes for which God created you? that your life on earth had not glorified him? that perhaps, you had lived someone else's life or someone else's idea of what your life should have been?

That won't happen if you take time each week to reflect and, if necessary, readjust your course. Researchers surveyed people over the age of ninety, asking them what they would do differently if they could live their lives over again. One of the top three answers was "I would reflect more." In other words, they would stop in more often at those checkpoints.

I can't think of anything that has helped me more in my Christian life than taking that time for regular reflection—stopping in at those checkpoints—to make sure I am, indeed, running with perseverance the race that God has marked out for me.

As with daily Bible reading, this isn't some onerous task. It's quite simple. Make fifty-two photocopies of the Weekly Evaluation Worksheet and you'll be set for a year. Then, each week, set aside fifteen to thirty minutes on Sunday afternoons to quietly reflect. If weather permits, you might go to a park or just sit in your own porch swing. With an open heart and pen in hand, write the truth about who you are and the way you're living.

I promise, it will transform you.

Take some time, right now, to answer the questions posed on the worksheet.

Incidentally, in case you're wondering what the other top two answers in the longevity survey were:

1. I would risk more.
2. I would do more significant things.

I think as we learn to walk in Total God-Confidence, we will become people who "risk more" and "do more significant things." With a little reflection mixed in, we'll have no regrets when we come to the end of our race.

Weekly Evaluation Worksheet

Week ending: _____

1. Am I listening for and hearing God's voice? What is he saying to me: through his Word, through prayer, through mature Christian believers, even through my circumstances?

2. Am I increasingly manifesting the fruits of the Holy Spirit: love, joy, peace, patience, kindness, goodness, faithfulness, gentleness, and self-control? What areas look encouraging? What needs prayer?

3. What did God teach me in my quiet times?

4. Am I on track with my read-through-the-Bible program? What am I learning?

5. Which priorities did I live by?

6. Which priorities did I neglect?

7. What new thing did I learn—about God, life, my family, and the people around me?

8. What are my specific priorities for the coming week?

Take Time to Reflect

1. Do you think you spend enough time reflecting upon your life?

2. How do you think you'd live differently if you did take time to reflect?

3. Take time to complete a Weekly Evaluation Worksheet.

4. Write out a prayer, asking God to give you his perspective on how well you are running your race.

5. What key lesson did you glean from today's study?

6. Write out This Week's Verse from memory.

Confidence Boosters:

- Don't skip life's checkpoints.
- Take time each week to reflect on how you're living your life.

Weekly Review:

See if you can fill in the ten characteristics of walking in Total God-Confidence. Look in the back of the book if you need help.

C _____ according to his purpose

O _____ to his plan

N _____ by his love

F _____ from the chains that bind

I _____ conformed to his character

D _____ in his Word

E _____ by faith

N _____ shaken by the jerks

C _____ that he is able and faithful

E _____ to take the leap of faith

WEEK SEVEN:

Energized
by Faith

This Week's Verse:

Being confident of this, that he who began a good work in
you will carry it on to completion until
the day of Christ Jesus.

Philippians 1:6 (NIV)

Day One

The Basis of Our Confidence

*For the Lord God, the Holy One of Israel, says: Only in re-
turning to me and waiting for me will you be saved; in quietness
and confidence is your strength.* Isaiah 30:15

I wonder what you're going through as you read these words. Is
life good for you right now? Is it everything you hoped it would be?
Do you have every cause for confidence? Or are you in the middle
of tough times? Financial difficulties, marriage conflicts, children in
trouble? If you're like most of the women I encounter, you have your
share of hardships and heartaches. As a result, on some level, your
confidence has been shaken.

No matter how complex your difficulties, I believe the solution
is simple: knowing God. He alone is the basis of our confidence.
When we don't know him, when we have an inaccurate picture of
who he is and what he can do, we allow the storms of life to overtake
us.

Here's how Andrew Murray puts it:

The great lack of our Christianity today is, *we do not know
God*. The answer to every complaint of weakness and failure, the
message to every congregation or convention seeking instruction
on holiness, should simply be: *Where is your God?* If you really
believe in God, he will put it all right. God is willing and able
by his Holy Spirit. Stop expecting the solution from yourself, or
the answer from anything there is in man, and simply yield yourself completely to God to work in you. . . .

Pray to God that we might get some right conception of what
influence could be made by a life spent, not in thought, or imag-

ination, or effort, but in the power of the Holy Spirit, wholly waiting upon God.[1]

I'm not saying that if you want a peanut butter and jelly sandwich, you should sit in your room and pray God will make you one. I *am* suggesting that making those PB&J sandwiches day after day would be less tedious if, while you did the work, you set your heart on God.

I am suggesting that, as we live our lives before him, confident that he knows exactly where we are, what we're doing, and *why* he has us doing it, we can walk in joy and confidence. Our answer to "Where is your God?" must continually be "He's right here with me." He's in the midst of the mess, in the midst of the storm. He's also on the beach and the roller coaster ride. I even found him there when I kissed my children good-night yesterday. And he's not standing idly by as I walk through my day, wringing his hands, hoping against hope that life will turn out okay for me. He's active and involved. I have complete confidence that everything that comes my way has either been sent or allowed by a God who is both all-loving and all-powerful.

Leonard Ravenhill noted that "No Christian is greater than his prayer life."[2] Your confidence cannot climb higher than the depths of your prayer life. We're not talking about "God, bless this mess" prayers. I mean prayer that aligns our heart with the purposes of God; prayer that enables us to know him better and, therefore, trust him more. As we grow in that knowledge and trust, we become more like him. Fundamentally, prayer doesn't change God; it changes us.

The basis of our confidence is the character of God. We serve a God who knows how to give good gifts to his children. I once heard a beautiful word picture of prayer: Prayer is like the gathering of gifts. We enter into the throne room of God and he is waiting there with good gifts he longs to give—to us, to those we love, and to the world at large. We approach the throne, and God fills

[1]Andrew Murray, *The Believer's Secret of Waiting on God* (Minneapolis: Bethany House Publishers, 1986), 14.
[2]Leonard Ravenhill, *God's Little Instruction Book on Prayer* (Tulsa: Honor Books, 1996), 26.

our arms with gifts, which we take back and give to those around us.

God knows what you need. He knows what your husband, your children, and your church need. Not only does he know our needs, we can have complete confidence that he is *both able and eager* to fill those needs, according to his riches in glory.

Whatever you need today, go to the throne room and gather the gifts he has waiting there for you.

Take Time to Reflect

1. Where is your God?

2. Describe your prayer life.

3. Write out a prayer asking God to fill your heart with good gifts to give others.

4. What key lesson did you glean from today's study?

5. Turn to the back of the book and remove your Bible verse card for this week.

Confidence Boosters:

• The solution to every problem is knowing God.
• Prayer is like the gathering of gifts, which we can then pass on to others.

Day Two

Aligning Your Life With the Purposes of God

Glorify your name, not ours, O Lord!   Psalm 115:1 TLB

When we speak of God-Confidence, what do we mean? What exactly can we be confident of? Can we be confident that things will always go our way? Confident that we'll always be happy, healthy, and wealthy? Confident that life will always be comfortable and convenient? Confident that God is "our butler, who art in heaven" to do our bidding?

No, but we can be confident of this: that if we will yield our will to God, he will be glorified through our lives. And if we can be completely confident of that one thing, then nothing else matters. That's because the whole purpose of our existence, the reason we're on this planet, is that we might *glorify* God. What does that mean? To *glorify* means "to accurately reflect his image."

Let's look at an example from the Bible:

Inside the tent the Lord spoke to Moses face to face, as a man speaks to his friend. Afterwards Moses would return to the camp, but the young man who assisted him, Joshua (son of Nun), stayed behind in the Tabernacle. Moses talked there with the Lord and said to him, "You have been telling me, 'Take these people to the Promised Land,' but you haven't told me whom you will send with me. You say you are my friend, and that I have found favor before you; please, if this is really so, guide me clearly along the way you want me to travel so that I will understand you and walk acceptably before you. For don't forget that this nation is your people."

And the Lord replied, "I myself will go with you and give you success."

For Moses had said, "If you aren't going with us, don't let us move a step from this place. If you don't go with us, who will ever know that I and my people have found favor with you, and that we are different from any other people upon the face of the earth?"

And the Lord had replied to Moses, "Yes, I will do what you have asked, for you have certainly found favor with me, and you are my friend" (Exodus 33:11–17).

As we seek to lead lives that glorify God, we can glean a number of significant lessons from this passage. Moses could walk in Total God-Confidence because:

- He had a personal relationship with God. He *knew* his God, because he took time to meet with him daily. Do you know your God? Do you take time to meet with him daily?
- He knew, without a shadow of a doubt, exactly what God had said. He was able to recall God's specific promises. How about you? Do you know what God has said in his Word? Are you able to stand on specific promises?
- He asked for guidance. Do you ask for guidance each day? Or do you walk according to your own whim? If you are unclear of God's direction for your life, could it be simply that you "have not because you ask not"? If you want to walk in Total God-Confidence, ask God for specific guidance.
- He asked *with the right motives*. Was Moses asking for a Mercedes Benz or an easy life? No, he asked, "that I will understand you and walk acceptably before you." If you ask God for understanding, with a goal toward walking acceptably in his sight, you can be completely confident that he will answer.
- God's glory is foremost in his mind. Moses says, "Don't forget, this nation is your people." He knows that a watching world will make judgments about who God is based on what they see in the lives of his people. He is concerned that Israel provide an *accurate reflection* of God. Is God's glory foremost in your mind?
- He didn't want what God didn't want for him. This simple truth has been revolutionary for me: if God doesn't want me to go somewhere, then why on earth would I want to go? If God doesn't want me to have something, then why on earth would I want to have it? If God doesn't want a certain person to be

part of my life, why cling to that person? What a liberating moment it was when I finally said, "Lord, I only want whatever you want me to want!" Can you make that the prayer of your heart today? If so, then you, like Moses, can walk in Total God-Confidence.

Take Time to Reflect

1. What does it mean to "glorify" God?

2. How accurately are you reflecting him?

3. Recount five lessons from the passage on Moses.

4. Look up Hebrews 12:1–2 and note God's word of encouragement.

5. What key lesson did you glean from today's study?

Confidence Boosters:

- Our sole purpose is to glorify God.
- To *glorify God* means to give an accurate reflection of who he is.

Day Three

Our Hearts' Desire

O Lord, we love to do your will! Our hearts' desire is to glorify your name.   Isaiah 26:8 TLB

What do you love to do more than anything else?

What is the deepest desire of your heart?

As you look within, can you honestly say that you *love* to do God's will? Is it your deepest desire to glorify his name? God wants to bring you to a place where you can honestly answer a hearty yes to both questions. At the moment when your yes is genuine, you'll experience a joy and a freedom you've never known. When what matters most to us are the things that do, indeed, matter most, we'll live a quality of life few people even know exists.

A. W. Tozer has observed that "you are what you want most."[1] Ask your heart: What would you rather have than anything else in the world? Here's a hint: What you think about most reveals your true priorities, even if they are not your professed priorities.

Let's turn these questions on their heads for a moment. Why *wouldn't* you love to do God's will? Why *wouldn't* the deepest desire of your heart be to glorify him?

For years my heart was cluttered with desires: for attention, for fame, for love, for financial security, and a million other jumbled motives. My deepest desire was to be someone important.

As God sifted my heart and forced me to examine the driving forces in my life, I discovered that FEAR was at the root of all my desires:

- I desperately desired attention and fame, because I *feared* no one

---

[1] A. W. Tozer, *The Pursuit of God* (Camp Hill, Pa.: Christian Publications, 1982), 27.

would care whether I lived or died.

- I desired love, because I *feared* I was unlovable.
- I desired financial security, because I *feared* not having my needs met.
- Most of all, I desired to feel important, because I *feared* I didn't matter at all.

If you will carefully examine what drives you, I suspect you'll discover the same thing I did: that much of our lives are motivated by fear. I've discovered that the only way to conquer a fear is to replace it with a greater fear.

Snakes provide a great example. Let's say a rattlesnake suddenly appears, coiled and ready to strike. You are overcome with fear of that snake. Then you realize that your toddler is running directly into the path of the rattler. At that moment, your fear of the snake pales in the face of a greater fear: fear that your child will be harmed. The same woman who thought only of fleeing a few moments earlier is ready to do battle with the snake.

Your fear was replaced by a greater fear.

Or take Eve as an example. She, too, encountered a snake. She was, no doubt, afraid to eat the forbidden fruit and risk displeasing God. But that fear was overcome by a greater fear: the fear that God was holding out on her. The fear that, if she obeyed God, she would miss out on something this world had to offer her.

If our hearts are set on anything other than the things of God, my guess is that, somewhere deep within, we share the fear of Eve. The fear that, if we turn our lives completely over to God and give him the preeminence in our lives, we will miss out on what this world has to offer.

When you think about it, it comes back again to *knowing God*. When we know our God, we know he desires *every* good thing for us. That he would never withhold any blessing, any joy. When we have complete confidence in his love for us, our hearts will be free from fear because "perfect love casts out fear."

As children of God, we should have only one burning fear in our hearts: the fear of not glorifying God. The fear of missing out on the blessing of being used by him. The fear of living our lives, yet missing the very purpose for which he created us.

That is a joyous fear. And it's a fear that conquers all other fears.
I'm not exactly a pillar of the faith, but I can honestly say that, at this moment, what matters most to me is doing God's will. The deepest desire of my heart is to glorify his name. It's a beautiful place to be. You can get there. It's found along the journey to walking in Total God-Confidence.

Take Time to Reflect

1. What are some of your fears?

2. How would you live differently if your only fear was the fear that God would not be glorified through your life?

3. Look up Matthew 28:18–20 and note God's word of encourgement.

4. Write out a prayer asking God to deliver you from fear.

5. What key lesson did you glean from today's study?

Confidence Boosters:

- The only way to conquer a fear is to replace it with a greater fear.
- Only one thing is worthy of our fear: the fear that our lives would not glorify God.

Day Four

Nothing That's Happened to You Has Caught God by Surprise

Now I'm about to tread on truly dangerous territory: the sovereignty of God versus the responsibility of man. I have agonized over this issue during most of my Christian life. As mentioned, I managed to get myself into quite a mess within two months of becoming a Christian. And I always wondered: Have I gone so far that God can't make it right again?

Here's my conclusion, for whatever it's worth: I picture God's sovereign control over our lives like a broad highway. Down the center of the road is a line, representing God's perfect will for our lives. The closer we stay to the center, the more obedient and faithful we are, the more we experience God's blessings. However, we can choose to veer from one side of the road to the other. In fact, we can spend our entire Christian lives in the gravel along the side of the road. It won't be very pleasant, but God will let us go that far. Some of us, unfortunately, have gotten so comfortable in the gravel, we've forgotten all about the center line. We prefer to live dangerously, hanging over the edge of the cliff. Still, we're not out of God's care, not out of his sovereign plan.

At any moment, we can turn the wheel of our lives back over to God and he can begin pulling us back to center. Now, if we've been in the gravel long enough, getting back to center may take some doing on God's part! There may be a blown tire, plenty of skid marks, and the like, but he can do it.

Unfortunately, our tendency, when we find ourselves in the gravel, is to veer to the other side of the road. Or we throw the thing in reverse, hoping to backtrack and undo the damage. These efforts only make things worse. We need to *let go of the wheel and give God control*.

Nothing you've done and nothing that's happened to you has

caught God by surprise. It's not as if God is walking around in heaven, and one day happens to look down at the mess you've made of your life, and shouts, "YIKES! I didn't know that was going to happen to her. That changes everything. I'm pretty much the sovereign God of the universe, but when it comes to her life, I can't quite pull the whole thing together."

Actually, I like to picture God like this: He's up in heaven, with the angel Gabriel standing next to him. He gives Gabriel the old side elbow and says, "Watch this one! I'll show them what I can do, something only I can do."

There is much more at stake in our lives than our own comfort and convenience. People are watching us. Most of us recognize that. However, we rarely stop to consider that there are forces in the heavenlies watching, as well. We fail to realize that God wants to glorify himself, throughout all the universe, through the lives of his people. I believe it does God's heart good when he can say, with confidence, "Go ahead, Satan, take your best shot at my servant Donna. I can trust her. She'll love me even if I don't give her a new Mercedes Benz. She'll love me even when nothing in her life makes sense. She'll love me even when I am all she has left." (Check out Job 1:1–12.)

Can God trust you?

Will you hang in there through the tough times, so that God might be glorified in the end? Will you refuse to be fooled by mere circumstances, and maintain, instead, an eternal perspective?

Consider the Cross. Think about Jesus: rejected, mocked, beaten, nailed to a cross, put to death. Picture Satan strutting around, thinking he's won the victory. If you think Peter and John were surprised to find the empty tomb, you should have seen Satan. That's because God did the last thing anyone would have expected. When all seemed hopeless, he gave Gabriel the old side elbow and said, "Watch this." And up from the grave Christ arose!

Satan actually thinks he's got some of you beat today. He thinks you are completely defeated and there's not a thing God can do about it. Well, he's in for another surprise! That's because God is in the redemption business, and I believe he wants to do in your life something only he can do. He wants to pull you back to center. Will you have enough faith to let go of the wheel and let him do it?

Take Time to Reflect

1. Are you in the center of God's will? Or in the gravel?

2. Can God trust you?

3. Look up 1 Peter 5:6–11 and note God's word of encouragement for you today.

4. Write out a prayer asking God to take control of the steering wheel of your life.

5. What key lesson did you glean from today's study?

Confidence Boosters:

- Nothing that's happened to you has caught God by surprise.
- God wants to do something in your life that only he can do.

Day Five

Energized by Faith

Yesterday I talked about how God wants to do something in our lives that only he can do. Normally when I talk like that, what I'm thinking of is big stuff. Giant leaps of faith, life-changing events, that sort of thing. But I've realized that it often takes more faith to plod day by day than it does to face large obstacles or undertake grand causes. That's because the energy to do "great things for God" can come from many sources besides faith. For example, we might be energized by the thrill of boosting our own ego. We might be energized by the hope of applause, excitement, or what have you.

When people hear me speaking, they often tell me they are amazed at my energy level. But let me be brutally honest. Some of that energy is from the Holy Spirit, some of it is Donna Partow energized by faith . . . but some of the energy is from other, less admirable sources.

The truth is, I absolutely love speaking to large audiences. And as far as I'm concerned, the larger the better. It's so exciting. Believe me, when I'm standing on a stage in front of four thousand women, I don't need faith to energize me. The electricity in the air and my skyrocketing adrenaline is enough.

Then one day after the crowds had gone home and I sat quietly in an airport, I felt my energy fading away. It was then I realized: *It is always like this when I am heading home.* Invariably, the minute I would walk through my front door my energy level would hit rock bottom. Funny how I could be so energetic among strangers, yet so lethargic with my own family.

At that moment, God laid a challenge on my heart. He asked me to devote myself to doing "smaller things with greater faithfulness." What I really needed was to be energized by faith in my daily routine. On New Year's Eve 1998 my family arrived late to the special evening service. The only seats left were in the front row. As I sat in the third seat in from the center aisle, the pastor asked each of us to pray for a major miracle in our lives. He challenged us to ask boldly. We all bowed our heads to pray for our great miracle. *Lord, what should I ask for?* I wondered. *To be part of some giant women's conference? To write a bestselling book?*

He replied, *"Ask me to give you strength. . . . to do smaller things with greater faithfulness."* Right then and there, I made my New Year's resolution: to humbly serve my husband and children with all the energy God supplies. Believe me, it's going to take a major miracle for that to happen!

It takes great faith to get out of bed every day and go about the mundane tasks of life in a spirit that honors our Father. It takes great faith to pursue holiness in our private lives, in our hearts and minds, where no one else can see. It takes great faith to persevere when we have every justification to quit. It's in those moments, in the midst of the small stuff, that we most need to be *energized by faith*.

> *Whoever wants to become great among you must be your servant, and whoever wants to be first must be slave of all. For even the Son of Man did not come to be served, but to serve, and to give his life as a ransom for many.* (Mark 10:43–45 NIV)

Take Time to Reflect

1. When do you have the greater need to be energized by faith: to do "big stuff" or in the small things?

2. Is there an area of your life where you have become lethargic? Write out a prayer asking God to energize you.

3. Is there some area of your life in which God is calling you to do "smaller things with greater faithfulness"?

4. What key lesson did you glean from today's study?

5. Write out This Week's Verse from memory.

Confidence Boosters:

- Sometimes it takes more faith to plod.
- God may be calling you to do "smaller things with greater faithfulness."

Weekly Review:

See if you can fill in the ten characteristics of walking in Total God-Confidence. Look in the back of the book if you need help.

C_____ according to his purpose

O_____ to his plan

N_____ by his love

F_____ from the chains that bind

I _____ conformed to his character

D_____ in his Word

E_____ by faith

N_____ shaken by the jerks

C_____ that he is able and faithful

E_____ to take the leap of faith

WEEK EIGHT:

Not Shaken by the Jerks

This Week's Verse:

But blessed is the man who trusts in the Lord and has made the Lord his hope and confidence.

Jeremiah 17:7

Day One

God Is Bigger Than the Jerks

This week I want to share with you a spiritual insight that you will not find revealed elsewhere in the annals of Christendom. It took me seventeen years to figure out this insight, which is so profound I'm thinking about printing T-shirts with this slogan emblazoned on them:

God is bigger than the jerks.

Well, what do you think?

What's that? You want to place an order?

I must confess how the Lord revealed this to me: through my husband. Although I respect him, I simply cannot deny that because of his Middle Eastern culture and some unresolved issues from his childhood, he sometimes acted like a real jerk.

But a whole planet full of jerks cannot thwart God's plan for our lives. Do you know that? God is in control. See, I always thought that God had a plan, but the jerks came along and blew the whole thing to pieces. Now don't get me wrong. I'm not saying God deliberately sends the jerks. No, not at all. God does not send the jerks, but he sure puts them to good use molding our character.

Maybe your husband, or your kids, or your parents, or your boss, or people in your church are acting like real jerks. And you think: *How can I be what God wants me to be when they're standing in the way?*

Philippians 1:6 says we can be confident of this: "that he who began a good work in you will carry it on to completion." There's not a jerk in the world who can prevent God from carrying that good work to completion. And what exactly *is* that good work?

It's the work of transforming our character. God's purpose for our lives is that we would truly become women of virtue. His ultimate plan for our lives has very little to do with our circumstances. Those are just the tools he uses to transform us into a vessel he can use. Whether it's physical illness or financial difficulties, whether you're single and wish you were married, or married and wish you were single—the circumstances aren't the point.

And by the way, God's ultimate plan has nothing to do with our convenience, although you wouldn't think so by looking at most of our prayer lists. It has to do with our character. And there's nothing quite like a jerk to drive us to our knees as we allow God to transform us from the inside out. As you can see, jerks actually play a vital role in our spiritual growth.

Let's hear it for the jerks.

All kidding aside. I want to talk with you very personally for a moment. Chances are, if you've been on the planet for more than a week, you've encountered a jerk. Someone who has hurt you very deeply. Someone who has hurt you over and over. And you're harboring that right to be hurt like a prized possession.

It's time to let it go.

It's time to forgive.

Now you're objecting: "If you knew what a jerk he was, you wouldn't ask me to forgive." You're absolutely right. I don't know. But God does and he is the one asking you to forgive. Forgive because God first forgave you. Forgive because forgiving doesn't make them right, forgiving sets you free. Forgive because it cleanses the bitterness, and God cannot use a vessel filled with bitterness.

I've also observed that the motivating force behind most jerks is their desire to control. They want power over you. Now think about this for a moment: As long as you don't forgive, they are in control. As long as you don't forgive, you're giving them exactly what they wanted in the first place.

Forgive, and give God control of your life again.

Take Time to Reflect

1. Do you have a jerk in your life? Describe what effect you've allowed him or her to have upon your life.

2. What are the implications in your life of the "profound spiritual insight" that God is bigger than the jerks?

3. Whom do you need to forgive?

4. Look up Matthew 18:21–22 and note God's word of instruction for you.

5. Write out a prayer asking God to help you forgive.

6. What key lesson did you glean from today's study?

7. Turn to the back of the book and remove your Bible verse card for this week.

Confidence Boosters:

- God is bigger than the jerks.
- Forgiving doesn't make the jerk right; forgiving sets you free.
- Forgive, and give God control of your life.

Day Two

Don't Let the Jerks Get the Best of You

Tomorrow I'm going to reveal my top-secret theory concerning the purpose behind jerks. Now, don't peek! First, I want you to read about a guy who was surrounded by jerks and draw your own conclusions.

> But when [Joseph's brothers] saw him coming, recognizing him in the distance, they decided to kill him!
>
> "Here comes that master-dreamer," they exclaimed. "Come on, let's kill him and toss him into a well and tell Father that a wild animal has eaten him. Then we'll see what will become of all his dreams!"
>
> But Reuben hoped to spare Joseph's life. "Let's not kill him," he said; "we'll shed no blood—let's throw him alive into this well here; that way he'll die without our touching him!" (Reuben was planning to get him out later and return him to his father.) So when Joseph got there, they pulled off his brightly colored robe, and threw him into an empty well—there was no water in it. Then they sat down for supper. Suddenly they noticed a string of camels coming towards them in the distance, probably Ishmaelite traders who were taking gum, spices, and herbs from Gilead to Egypt.
>
> "Look there," Judah said to the others. "Here come some Ishmaelites. Let's sell Joseph to them! Why kill him and have a guilty conscience? Let's not be responsible for his death, for, after all, he is our brother!" And his brothers agreed. So when the traders came by, his brothers pulled Joseph out of the well and sold him to them for twenty pieces of silver, and they took him along to Egypt. (Genesis 37:18–28)
>
> When Joseph arrived in Egypt as a captive of the Ishmaelite traders, he was purchased from them by Potiphar, a member of the personal staff of Pharaoh, the king of Egypt. Now this man

Potiphar was the captain of the king's bodyguard and his chief executioner. The Lord greatly blessed Joseph there in the home of his master, so that everything he did succeeded. Potiphar noticed this and realized that the Lord was with Joseph in a very special way. So Joseph naturally became quite a favorite with him. Soon he was put in charge of the administration of Potiphar's household, and all of his business affairs. At once the Lord began blessing Potiphar for Joseph's sake. All his household affairs began to run smoothly, his crops flourished and his flocks multiplied. So Potiphar gave Joseph the complete administrative responsibility over everything he owned. He hadn't a worry in the world with Joseph there, except to decide what he wanted to eat! Joseph, by the way, was a very handsome young man.

One day at about this time Potiphar's wife began making eyes at Joseph, and suggested that he come and sleep with her.

Joseph refused. "Look," he told her, "my master trusts me with everything in the entire household; he himself has no more authority here than I have! He has held back nothing from me except you yourself because you are his wife. How can I do such a wicked thing as this? It would be a great sin against God."

But she kept on with her suggestions day after day, even though he refused to listen, and kept out of her way as much as possible. Then one day as he was in the house going about his work—as it happened, no one else was around at the time—she came and grabbed him by the sleeve demanding, "Sleep with me." He tore himself away, but as he did, his jacket slipped off and she was left holding it as he fled from the house. When she saw that she had his jacket, and that he had fled, she began screaming; and when the other men around the place came running in to see what had happened, she was crying hysterically. "My husband had to bring in this Hebrew slave to insult us!" she sobbed. "He tried to rape me, but when I screamed, he ran, and forgot to take his jacket."

She kept the jacket, and when her husband came home that night, she told him her story. "That Hebrew slave you've had around here tried to rape me, and I was only saved by my screams. He fled, leaving his jacket behind!"

Well, when her husband heard his wife's story, he was furious. He threw Joseph into prison, where the king's prisoners were kept in chains. But the Lord was with Joseph there, too, and was kind to him by granting him favor with the chief jailer. (Genesis 39:1–21)

The wine taster told his dream first. "In my dream," he said, "I saw a vine with three branches that began to bud and blossom, and soon there were clusters of ripe grapes. I was holding Pharaoh's wine cup in my hand, so I took the grapes and squeezed the juice into it, and gave it to him to drink."

"I know what the dream means," Joseph said. "The three branches mean three days! Within three days Pharaoh is going to take you out of prison and give you back your job as his wine taster. And please have some pity on me when you are back in his favor, and mention me to Pharaoh, and ask him to let me out of here. For I was kidnapped from my homeland among the Hebrews, and now this—here I am in jail when I did nothing to deserve it."

Pharaoh's birthday came three days later, and he held a party for all of his officials and household staff. He sent for his wine taster and chief baker, and they were brought to him from the prison. Then he restored the wine taster to his former position. . . . Pharaoh's wine taster, however, promptly forgot all about Joseph, never giving him a thought. (Genesis 40:9–15, 20–21, 23)

"I am Joseph!" he said to his brothers. "Is my father still alive?" But his brothers couldn't say a word, they were so stunned with surprise. "Come over here," he said. So they came closer. And he said again, "I am Joseph, your brother whom you sold into Egypt! But don't be angry with yourselves that you did this to me, for God did it! He sent me here ahead of you to preserve your lives. These two years of famine will grow to seven, during which there will be neither plowing nor harvest. God has sent me here to keep you and your families alive, so that you will become a great nation. Yes, it was God who sent me here, not you! And he has made me a counselor to Pharaoh, and manager of this entire nation, ruler of all the land of Egypt" (Genesis 45:3–8).

Then Joseph returned to Egypt with his brothers and all who had accompanied him to the funeral of his father. But now that their father was dead, Joseph's brothers were frightened.

"Now Joseph will pay us back for all the evil we did to him," they said. So they sent him this message: "Before he died, your father instructed us to tell you to forgive us for the great evil we did to you. We servants of the God of your father beg you to forgive us." When Joseph read the message, he broke down and cried.

Then his brothers came and fell down before him and said, "We are your slaves."

But Joseph told them, "Don't be afraid of me. Am I God, to judge and punish you? As far as I am concerned, God turned into good what you meant for evil, for he brought me to this high position I have today so that I could save the lives of many people. No, don't be afraid. Indeed, I myself will take care of you and your families." And he spoke very kindly to them, reassuring them.

So Joseph and his brothers and their families continued to live in Egypt. Joseph was 110 years old when he died. (Genesis 50:14–22)

Take Time to Reflect

1. Circle the names of all the jerks Joseph encounters.

2. How does Joseph refuse to let the jerks get the best of him?

3. Who is really in control? The jerks . . . or God? Underline evidences of God's sovereignty.

4. Are the jerks able to thwart God's plan for Joseph's life? Circle evidence that they are *not*.

5. How does Joseph treat the jerks in the end? Does he seek revenge or does he forgive?

6. What key lesson did you glean from today's study?

Confidence Boosters:

- A whole planet full of jerks cannot thwart what God wants to accomplish through your life.
- If you don't want the jerks to get the best of you, stay focused on the sovereignty of God.

Day Three

The Purpose of Jerks

If I were to choose the defining characteristic of a jerk, I'd probably have to say they're annoying. (I hasten to add that not all annoying people are full-fledged jerks; that is, they are not malicious.) Nevertheless, I've found that annoying people play a vital role in our lives: they reveal our sin. Let me give you an example. I homeschool. (You either applauded or thought, *That is seriously weird.*) I often say, "If it weren't for my kids, I would love homeschooling. And if it weren't for homeschooling, I would love my kids."

Mind you, my kids aren't genuine jerks, but the mere fact that we're together twenty-four hours a day causes me to find them . . . dare I say it? Annoying. It's tempting to think, *If I could just ship these kids off to boarding school, I would be a saint.* (Wait a minute: boarding school?!?! Not a bad idea.) It's tempting to point the finger at the little urchins and yell, "You kids are making me sin."

You want to know the truth, though? The awful truth? The glorious truth? They're not making me sin. They're just revealing the sin that's already there.

Think about that for a minute.

Maybe you've been telling yourself, *If I had a different husband, I would be the perfect wife. If I had different kids, I'd be the mother of the year. If I had a different boss, I'd be a great employee.* However, we're just deceiving ourselves. The truth is, we're sinners in need of repentance. A different husband might make our lives less tumultuous, but it wouldn't do a thing to change the condition of our heart.

The purpose of jerks—and just plain, ordinary, annoying people—is to cleanse us from sin. Here's how it works:

1. *Reveal.* The first step to cleansing is revelation. You can't be cleansed of a sin if you don't know it exists. So, the jerks and annoying people do you a great favor when they reveal the sin within.

2. *Confess.* The next step is vitally important once the sin is revealed, we must confess it. As far as I have been able to determine, nowhere in the Bible does God promise to forgive unconfessed sin. Remember 1 John 1:9: "If we confess our sins, he is faithful and just and will forgive us our sins and purify us from all unrighteousness." Which do you think is the most important word in that verse? In my opinion, it's that tiny two-letter word "if."

3. *Cleanse.* Once the jerks have done their part in revealing our sin; once we've done our part in confessing our sin; then, and only then, can God do his part in cleansing the sin.

Now I want you to sit down and write a thank-you note to the most annoying person you know. You don't have to lie. Just write, "I want to thank you for the vital role you're playing in my spiritual growth."

Yesterday I declared that "God doesn't send the jerks, but he sure puts them to good use molding our character." After searching the Bible more thoroughly, I think I need to amend that statement.

You have three assignments as you read through the following passage: First, see if you can identify the jerk. Second, see if you can determine where the jerk came from. Third, see if you can discover the purpose of the jerk! You might be surprised by the answers!

> *But I will cause Pharaoh to stubbornly refuse, and I will multiply my miracles in the land of Egypt.* (Exodus 7:3)
>
> *This time I am going to send a plague that will really speak to you and to your servants and to all the Egyptian people, and prove to you there is no other God in all the earth. I could have killed you all by now, but I didn't, for I wanted to demonstrate my power to you and to all the earth.* (Exodus 9:14–16)
>
> *The Lord had told Moses, "Pharaoh won't listen, and this will give me the opportunity of doing mighty miracles to demonstrate my power"* (Exodus 11:9).
>
> *And once again I will harden Pharaoh's heart and he will chase after you. I have planned this to gain great honor and glory over Pharaoh and all his armies, and the Egyptians shall know that I am the Lord"* (Exodus 14:4).
>
> *I will harden the hearts of the Egyptians and they will go in after you and you will see the honor I will get in defeating Pharaoh and all his armies, chariots, and horsemen. And all Egypt shall*

know that I am Jehovah" (Exodus 14:17–18).

What answers did you come up with? Here are mine:
1. The jerk is Pharaoh.
2. God deliberately sent the jerk.
3. God did so to glorify himself and to demonstrate his power.
I know this is radical stuff, but study the Scriptures for yourself.

> *For the Scripture says to Pharaoh: "I raised you up for this very purpose, that I might display my power in you and that my name might be proclaimed in all the earth." Therefore God has mercy on whom he wants to have mercy, and he hardens whom he wants to harden.*
>
> *What if God, choosing to show his wrath and make his power known, bore with great patience the objects of his wrath—prepared for destruction? What if he did this to make the riches of his glory known to the objects of his mercy, whom he prepared in advance for glory?* (Romans 9:17–18, 22–23 NIV)

There you have it, folks. God not only sends the jerks, he carefully fashions them so that he can do . . . what? Display his power in you. When you refuse to let the jerks get the best of you, you display God's power. When, through your life, you declare that God's glory means more than your convenience, his mighty name is proclaimed in all the earth.

Now make it personal:

- Who's the jerk in your life?
- Who sent him/her?
- Why did God send him/her?

Here are two more important questions:

- Will you display God's power?
- Will you, by your life, declare his glory?

Take Time to Reflect

1. Who's the jerk in your life?

2. How can you glorify God through your relationship with that jerk?

3. Write out a prayer expressing your desire to glorify God through your difficult relationship(s).

4. What key lesson did you glean from today's study?

Confidence Boosters:

- Sometimes God *does* send the jerks!
- When we respond with Total God-Confidence, we display God's power and bring glory to his name.

Day Four

Love 'em All, and Let God Sort 'em Out

Now, I've shared my marriage story with enough audiences to know that rather than pondering the profound spiritual truths I've been revealing, most of you are sitting there thinking, *What on earth happened with her husband?*

You nosy bunch! I'll bet you subscribe to *The National Enquirer*, too! Now, I could devote an entire book to my marriage. The Drama. The Intrigue. Instead, I'm going to cover it quickly. Here's what we will do: I'll let you vote for the ending! Vote for how you think the story ends . . . or how you think it *should have ended*. You can vote for one of the following:

1. I woke up one morning and realized, "Hey, I'm a princess. I don't have to put up with this stuff. No more, no way, no how! See ya!" With that, I promptly walked out.

Okay, how many of you voted for #1? Good guess, but wrong. We're still married. In fact, we recently celebrated our seventeenth wedding anniversary. Let's try again.

2. My husband suddenly became a Christian and "poof!" he was magically transformed into a giant of the faith.

Raise your hand if you like that one.

Another popular guess, but I'm afraid you're wrong again. He made a very genuine profession of faith before we were married and was a churchgoing, Bible-study-attending Christian throughout the entire ordeal. In fact, if we conducted "fruit inspections," he would have come out with a seal of approval.

You're running out of options, ladies. Let's try one more:

3. Seventeen years ago, I walked down an aisle wearing my mother's wedding gown. I stood before God, and said, "I'll stick with this man, for better or for worse, till death do us part." And that's what I did.

Ding . . . ding . . . ding . . . ding . . . ding. You've just won the grand prize!

Having just read option #3, you probably have one of two reactions. First, you responded, "Hey, wait a minute. Is she saying I shouldn't have divorced *my* husband? Is she saying divorce is always wrong? I knew there was something about this chick I didn't like."

RELAX! This is not a book about divorce and remarriage. Gee, you gals can be t-o-u-c-h-y! I'm sharing what God called me to do; he may or may not be calling you to do the same thing. I don't know your circumstances and I'm not going to tell you *everything* about mine. But trust me, divorce was never a serious option.

The rest of you are probably thinking, *Oh, that Donna is a saint. She must be the most amazing Christian in the entire world to survive such an ordeal. If only I could live in her neighborhood, I know we'd be best friends.*

No, I'm not a saint. If you heard my husband's side of the story, I'm sure he'd tell you I can dish it out as well as take it. Before you get me too high on a pedestal, I'd better make a confession: *I prayed almost daily that my husband would get in a car accident.*

I wasn't malicious. In fact, I'd pray, "Dear God, you know I can't take another day of this, but he's not a completely horrible person. So here's what I suggest: a quick, painless car accident."

You probably won't believe this, but I have the insurance records to prove it: My husband walked away from three should-have-been-fatal car accidents. He fell asleep at the wheel on the New Jersey turnpike, crashing into the concrete barricade at 60 miles per hour . . . and walked away. Then, he was hit by a drunk driver. His car spun around and crashed, head-on, into a steel light post. The car was completely totaled. He walked away. Most recently, he inadvertently pulled out in front of a truck, which crashed into him, completely totaling his Volvo. It takes a whole lot to total a Volvo. Once again, my husband literally walked away. I found him wandering down a highway, in shock, about five miles from the accident scene.

I'm slow to catch on, but even I can take the hint. So after the last car accident, I remembered a T-shirt I once saw that read, *Kill 'em all and let God sort 'em out.* I decided to adopt it as my motto . . . with one slight variation: *Love 'em all and let God sort 'em out.*

I interpreted the three car accidents as God's way of saying, "I *could have . . .* but I didn't." I figured, as long as God keeps my husband around, there must be a reason. It's not my job to change my husband. It's my job to love him.

And I do love my husband. If you ever meet him, you will adore him. Everyone does! He is an incredibly nice guy. As I often tell women, as long as he's not IN LOVE WITH YOU, you're pretty much okay. By the way, I think that should serve as an excellent deterrent to any woman who may have designs on my husband.

We're working on our marriage, just like everyone else. It's been a long, slow, painful process. People often ask, "Was there a turning point?" At first I said no, but then I realized there *was*.

Do you remember week 3, day 4, "Awaiting the Rescue," where we discovered that Rahab waited for God to rescue her? She didn't develop a contingency plan. She didn't try to rescue herself. (If you don't remember, reread it!)

Well, I was like Rahab, sitting there, looking out the window, waiting for God to deliver me. The first year passed. *Uh-oh. I've made some big mistakes in my life, but this one is sleeping next to me. Permanently.* The second year. *God's bound to show up any day now. He knows I can't take much more of this.* The third year. *I'll bet he lost my address!* The fourth year. The fifth. Six, seven, eight, nine, ten years passed, and I thought help would never come.

Then, eight years ago, I gave birth to my first child. She was afflicted with colic, which caused her to scream day and night. The only thing that comforted her was—get ready for this—*walking around the block*.

Remember how Rahab's deliverance came? Yep, with an army *walking around the block*. Hey, if God ever tells you to walk around the block, GO. Your deliverance is drawing near!

From those first walks around the block with Leah, I began taking trips to the grocery store, then the mall. Then I began traveling around the country with my family. In 1997 I began traveling alone to retreat centers across the United States. Things have gotten better and better to the point where my life is ALMOST normal. Of course, with me in the middle of it, how normal can it get?

I think there's a lesson in this for all of us. If you're single, *don't date an Iranian*. If you have a good marriage, be thankful. Go give your husband a great big hug! Then resolve to do all you can to make your marriage even better.

If you're in a tough marriage, hang in there. Allow those trials to cleanse you so that God might be glorified through your life.

I do want to say a word to the woman who may be reading this who is in a *dangerous* marriage. God is not asking you to hang around and be a punching bag for some jerk. You need to get help, but don't do anything rash. You don't want to "set him off." First, read *The Excellent Wife* by Martha Peace[1], with special attention to chapter 14, "God's Provision for the Wife's Protection." I don't want you to skip the first thirteen chapters, though. Those are critical. However, I do want to give you the bottom line: Your husband needs to see that it's not him against pathetic, helpless little you. He needs to know that it's him against *God. Plus* you have the entire church standing with you.

I'm not a big fan of divorce, but I'm a very big fan of separation, if it's done under the guidance and protection of the local church leadership. In other words, don't just run off and hide in a cheap motel. You'll make matters worse.

I was attending a conference on the East Coast when a pastor's wife came up to me and said, "I heard you speak a year ago and it totally changed my life!" I was wondering what spiritual insight I had imparted that was so life-changing. So I asked. To my surprise, she said, "When you said your husband acted like a jerk—I couldn't believe you admitted that! You should have seen the looks on women's faces. They were stunned, but they could totally identify. It was like a huge wave of relief flooded over us all. We realized, 'We're not alone!' It was great because my husband is a pastor. He's a wonderful, godly man, but I've got to tell you, sometimes he acts like a real *jerk.*"

I had always been nervous about using the "j" word. After one conference, I got a call from a woman who strongly objected. She said she even sensed some "latent, unresolved anger" toward my husband. I felt like saying, "Duh, the man held me hostage for ten years. I *might* have some unresolved issues left." So not only was I angry with my husband, I was angry with *her.* However, before she hung

---

[1]You can order the book by calling 770–486–0011.

up, she said the dreaded words, "I felt GOD wanted me to call you."
Uh-oh.

Now I had to wrestle with the implications: Was she just a jerk
complaining about my use of the word "jerk"? Or did God truly
prompt her to call me? Reluctantly, I began to pray. I was afraid God
might ask me to completely forgive my husband.

He did.

And I did.

Guess what? Forgiving didn't make him right; forgiving set me
free. Although it took me a long, long time to get to this place, I can
honestly say, "I have forgiven my husband."

Are there some "latent, unresolved" issues in your marriage or
other vital relationship? Take my advice: Let them go.

Take Time to Reflect

1. How would you rate your most vital relationship (whether it's a
   marriage, friendship, what have you)?

2. What principles can you apply from today's lesson, to improve that
   relationship?

3. Write out a prayer asking God to show you if you have any "latent,
   unresolved" issues you need to face. Ask God to help you forgive.

4. What key lesson did you glean from today's study?

Confidence Boosters:

- It's not our job to change our loved ones. It's our job to "love 'em all and let God sort 'em out."
- If you have latent, unresolved issues in a key relationship, it's time to let them go. It's time to forgive.

Day Five

What If You're Married to Him?

I realize some women reading this book are not married, but since many are, and since so many of us have husbands who at least occasionally act like jerks, I'd like to offer some friendly advice on dealing with a jerk, when the jerk sleeps next to you.

Advice #1: Give up any hope of changing your husband. It's impossible. If any woman in the world could have changed her husband, it would have been me. No matter how hard I tried, I couldn't do it. It's something only God can do.

Advice #2: Rather than focusing on the pursuit of happiness in your marriage, focus on the pursuit of holiness. Rather than asking God to change your husband, ask God to change YOU. When you become a different wife, you may find that your husband becomes a different man. Then again, he may be the same old jerk. That's not the point. God will be at work transforming your character. As a result, God will be glorified through your life. What else matters?

To help you along in the journey, I've developed a clever little formula. (I hope you're proud of me. I *rarely* come up with memorable formulas!) Ready? It's GAP. It's based on Ezekiel 22:30, where the Lord says, "I looked for a man among them who would build up the wall and stand before me in the gap on behalf of the land." God was looking for someone who would intercede on another's behalf. That's what we need to do as wives: stand in the gap, interceding on our husband's behalf.

Here's what GAP stands for:

GODLY wife. Whether he knows it or not, what your husband needs most is a godly wife. Nothing is more important to your marriage. Not great cooking or great decorating or a great big house, not even a great love life—although I'm sure your husband will appreciate all those things. Nothing money can buy, nothing you can learn or do or achieve, nothing is more important than your personal relationship with God.

I counsel with so many women whose marriages are in ruins. In every case, the real problem wasn't that her husband was a jerk (although a lot of the husbands were). The real problem was that the woman didn't know her God. I can say that without judgment, because there was a time when my marriage was in ruins. And when I sorted through the wreckage, I found that I had never really known my God. Never really understood all that he could be—all that he wanted to be—in my life.

Commit yourself to know the truth, the core doctrines of the faith. I can't tell you how many women have said to me, "Well, I know God wants me to be happy." When I hear words to that effect, I immediately know I'm dealing with a woman who doesn't know God's Word. More than our happiness, God wants our *holiness*. Don't ever be some wimpy woman who doesn't know her God! Be strong in your knowledge of the truth and secure in God's love and provision for you.

As mentioned before, a great resource to help you toward that goal is *The Excellent Wife* by Martha Peace. It is, without question, the most balanced, biblical book I've found on the subject of being a godly wife.

ADORING wife. Okay, now for the really challenging part: Your husband needs an adoring wife. One day I was praying that God would fix my husband. I cried out, "O God, you've seen how I've endured my husband all these years."

He replied, "Yeah, I've seen it. That's not the problem. The problem is that your *husband* has seen how you've endured him. No man wants to be endured. He wants to be adored. Don't endure your husband. Adore him."

WHAT??

Yep, adore him.

Here's what I did. I wrote down all the things I appreciated about my husband. In the beginning, I had to pad the list with stuff like "He doesn't play golf" and "He doesn't watch baseball on television." I quickly came up with twenty-seven items. Admittedly, some things were silly; but there were many truly wonderful things, too. Like his devotion to his family. His integrity. His sincere desire to put others before himself. Most of all, he is genuinely a *nice person* who cares about other people. As I began to sincerely praise my husband, I began to feel like an adoring wife! And he began to feel like an adored husband. It works, ladies. It works!

Here's my challenge to you. Begin an ongoing list of everything you adore about your husband. Make it a point to verbally acknowledge his positive characteristics or thoughtful deeds. Recall special moments you've shared together. Encourage character growth that you see in him. To make this project extra special, present your discoveries as a gift to your husband. Transfer all of the "adorable items" onto individual slips of paper. You can neatly write or type the slips. Then, decorate a jar or box. (If you're in a study group, you can decorate the containers together. Make it a fun project!) Next, arrange a special evening with your husband and present this to him, perhaps reading aloud the slips, one by one.

PRAYING wife. He may not tell you this, but another thing your husband needs is a praying wife. If you're anything like me, you haven't even begun to tap into the power of prayer to transform your husband. I'm embarrassed to admit this, but for most of my married life, the only prayer I ever prayed concerning my husband was "Get him away from me!" (I assume you remember the car accident scenario!) Or, possibly, "Change him, so my life will get better." I never prayed for him—*for his sake*. It never even occurred to me that God didn't want to change my husband; he wanted to change ME.

My husband is actually descended from Persian royalty (for those of you who don't know this, Iran is modern-day Persia). Believe it or not, we were together for sixteen years before the thought dawned on me that the book of Esther might have special significance for my life. Just because she was a believer married to Persian royalty, should this be relevant? Hello, Donna!

Esther had many wonderful qualities, but I want to focus on one: She was a praying wife. After her husband had issued the edict to kill all the Jews—which was basically a death warrant for his wife— Esther didn't just run into the throne room and tell him he was an idiot. She didn't wag her finger and say, "How could you be so stupid?" Or even, "How could you do this to me?"

She didn't go to her *husband's* throne room until she had gone into her *father's* throne room. That's a good rule for us to follow.

I also notice that Esther raised up prayer support; she asked others to approach the father's throne before she approached her husband's throne:

> *"Go, gather together all the Jews who are in Susa and fast for me. Do not eat or drink for three days, night or day. I and my maids will fast as you do. When this is done, I will go to the king, even though it is against the law. And if I perish, I perish"* (Esther 4:16 NIV).

Notice that she doesn't reveal any gory details about her marriage. She just asks for prayer. No one needs to know all the details about your marriage. There are always people in the church looking for morsels. Don't give them any. Those who truly love you will pray. Just say, "I need to talk with my husband about an important issue. And I'd appreciate your prayers." Enough said.

We have a choice when there's a conflict or difficulty in our marriage, about who we will turn to for counsel. We can take it to the throne or take it to the phone. I'll be the first to admit, one of the biggest mistakes I've made is taking it to the phone rather than the throne. My girlfriends can't change my husband. They can't even change their own husbands! They certainly can't change my heart toward my husband. Only God can do that.

Now let me clarify: You should have one mature, godly woman—a Titus 2 mentor—whom you turn to for counsel. However, you don't turn to the whole neighborhood. And your first recourse is always the throne: James 1:5 says, "If any of you lacks wisdom, he should ask God," not the woman down the street. He certainly gave Esther wisdom to deal with her husband, didn't he? He'll do the same for you.

When my dear husband gets on my nerves, I find strength in Hebrews 4:16:

> *Let us then approach the throne of grace with confidence, so that we may receive mercy and find grace to help us in our time of need.*

We can approach our father about our husband *anytime we want.* There we will receive mercy and grace. Let me encourage you to begin not only praying for your husband, but fasting as well. Why not follow Esther's lead and commit to a three-day fast? Involve several of your women friends in the fast. If you're doing this study as part of a group, I would strongly urge *all of you* to join in the fast.

Here's how I'd do it. Each of you write down *one thing* you want to discuss with your husband; something that's been bothering you for a long time. Keep this between you and the Lord. Pray and fast for one another for three days. At the end of that time, each of you approach your husband. Then, report back the results. By the way, I love Esther's idea of taking her husband out to dinner, setting the right mood for open discussion.

During your fast—and every other day for that matter—I suggest you use Stormie Omartian's book *The Power of a Praying Wife* (Harvest House) as your guide. It's a wonderful tool that will teach you exactly how to pray God's will for your husband. No wife should be without it.

So, when your husband acts like a real jerk, remember to stand in the GAP for him, being the kind of wife he needs:

- godly
- adoring
- praying

Even if it doesn't change your husband, I guarantee it will change you.

Take Time to Reflect

1. Write out a prayer for your husband.

2. When will you fast for your husband? Commit to a date.

3. Who will you ask to join you in your fast? List their names and contact them.

4. What *one* issue do you want to speak to your husband about? Write it below, but keep it confidential.

5. Begin the list of your husband's adorable qualities.

6. Make your jar or box (or at least make plans to make it).

7. When will you present your jar or box to your husband? Write some specific plans below.

8. What key lesson did you glean from today's study?

9. Write out This Week's Verse from memory.

Confidence Boosters:

- What your husband needs most is for you to stand in the GAP for him. He needs you to be a godly, adoring, praying wife.
- Perhaps God doesn't want to change your husband. He wants to change *you*.

Weekly Review:

See if you can fill in the ten characteristics of walking in Total God-Confidence. Look in the back of the book if you need help.

C _____ according to his purpose

O _____ to his plan

N _____ by his love

F _____ from the chains that bind

I _____ conformed to his character

D _____ in his Word

E _____ by faith

N _____ shaken by the jerks

C _____ that he is able and faithful

E _____ to take the leap of faith

WEEK NINE:
Convinced That
He Is Able and Faithful

This Week's Verse:

Your steadfast love, O Lord, extends to the heavens, your
faithfulness to the clouds.

Psalm 36:5 (NRSV)

Day One

Facing the Furnace

"If we are thrown into the flaming furnace, our God is able to deliver us; and he will deliver us out of your hand, Your Majesty. But if he doesn't, please understand, sir, that even then we will never under any circumstance serve your gods or worship the gold statue you have erected."　　　　　Daniel 3:17–18

Anyone who's spent more than a few weeks in Sunday school surely knows the story of Shadrach, Meshach, and Abednego, the three coolest teenagers in the Bible. On the off-chance that you don't remember, I'll sum it up. The King of Babylon set up a tall gold statue and ordered everyone to bow down and worship it. These three teenagers, who had been taken from their homes in Jerusalem, refused to obey the king's command. They wouldn't bow.

When they were told to either bow or burn, they responded with the ultimate God-confident slogan: "Our God is able . . . but even if he doesn't . . ." That's it! We've spent eight weeks trying to get to the heart of the matter, and these teenagers do it in two sentences.

We have to believe that he is able. Many Christians believe that. Unfortunately, too many follow that affirmation with a demand: "Therefore, he *has to.*" In other words, since God is *able* to heal me, *able* to give me a promotion, *able* to bless me with children, *able* to send me lots of money; since God is *able* to do all these things, then he better get cracking! And if he doesn't . . . they question his love and his faithfulness.

Then there's another category of Christians. They are the Christians who subscribe to the "even if he doesn't" portion of the God-confident slogan. They know God loves them; they're confident of that. They just don't think he's able to accomplish much in their daily lives. They're never bitterly disappointed in God, because they keep their expectations so low, any "god" could live up to them. They question his ability and his power.

Total God-Confidence requires both: confidence that he is able—that our God is an awesome God, active in the lives of his people. And confidence that he loves us, and that even when he says "No" he's still faithful.

Total God-Confidence declares, "God is able . . . but even if he doesn't, I'll still follow him."

Take Time to Reflect

1. Do you believe that God is able but doubt his love and faithfulness when he doesn't do what you ask?

2. Or are you more inclined to love God "even if he doesn't," mostly because you doubt he could even if he wanted to?

3. What situation are you facing right now that you need to face with an attitude that says, "God is able . . . but even if he doesn't . . ."?

4. Write out a prayer expressing your confidence that God is both able and faithful.

5. What key lesson did you glean from today's study?

6. Turn to the back of the book and remove your Bible verse card for this week.

Confidence Boosters:

- God is able to deliver us from any situation, but that doesn't mean he has to.
- We must love God "even if he doesn't," without ever doubting his ability to act with power.

Day Two

The Heart of the King

The king's heart is in the hand of the Lord; he directs it like a
watercourse wherever he pleases.　　　　　　　Proverbs 21:1 NIV

Hopefully, after yesterday, you are convinced that God is able to
deliver you from a pagan king. (In case you don't know how the story
ends: the king throws them into the fire, but they don't burn!) Unfortunately, your problem isn't with a pagan king, it's with that creepy
boss of yours (or your spouse's boss)! Surely God has no influence
over that godless fellow?!? Actually, the Bible says that God is in control of your job situation. He's in control of your *husband's* job situation, as well. I know how hard it is when you feel sure that you (or
your spouse) deserve so much more money, more credit, more pro-
motions, and if it weren't for that *creep*, you're confident God could
do something about the situation.

I'll admit, I have lived in torment over both my career and my
husband's. More precisely, the amount of income—or lack thereof—
derived from aforementioned illustrious careers! I would get so angry
at my boss, his boss, the "corporate world" at large. Why wouldn't
they pay us what we were worth? Then I found this verse:

> *For promotion and power come from nowhere on earth, but only*
> *from God. He promotes one and deposes another.* (Psalm 75:6)

God decides who gets promoted. God decides how much money
we make. God even decides whose ministry rises and falls. (Yeah, I've
gotten angry and frustrated about *that*, too!) Promotion is *only from*
God.

We find evidence of this throughout the Bible. Today we come
back to the life of Nehemiah, actually picking up his story a bit earlier

than we did in week 4. Read through the passage and see what characteristics of God-Confidence you can glean. Tomorrow I'll share my thoughts.

The autobiography of Nehemiah, the son of Hecaliah:

In December of the twentieth year of the reign of King Arta-xerxes of Persia, when I was at the palace at Shushan, one of my fellow Jews named Hanani came to visit me with some men who had arrived from Judah. I took the opportunity to inquire about how things were going in Jerusalem.

"How are they getting along?" I asked. "—the Jews who returned to Jerusalem from their exile here?"

"Well," they replied, "things are not good; the wall of Jerusalem is still torn down, and the gates are burned."

When I heard this, I sat down and cried. In fact, I refused to eat for several days, for I spent the time in prayer to the God of heaven.

"O Lord God," I cried out, "O great and awesome God who keeps his promises and is so loving and kind to those who love and obey him! Hear my prayer! Listen carefully to what I say! Look down and see me praying night and day for your people Israel. I confess that we have sinned against you; yes, I and my people have committed the horrible sin of not obeying the commandments you gave us through your servant Moses. Oh, please remember what you told Moses! You said,

" 'If you sin, I will scatter you among the nations; but if you return to me and obey my laws, even though you are exiled to the farthest corners of the universe, I will bring you back to Jerusalem. For Jerusalem is the place in which I have chosen to live.'

"We are your servants, the people you rescued by your great power. O Lord, please hear my prayer! Heed the prayers of those of us who delight to honor you. Please help me now as I go in and ask the king for a great favor—put it into his heart to be kind to me."
(I was the king's cupbearer.)

One day in April four months later, as I was serving the king his wine he asked me, "Why so sad? You aren't sick, are you? You look like a man with deep troubles." (For until then I had always been cheerful when I was with him.) I was badly frightened, but I replied, "Sir, why shouldn't I be sad? For the city where my ancestors are buried is in ruins, and the gates have been burned down."

"Well, what should be done?" the king asked. With a quick prayer to the God of heaven, I replied, "If it please Your Majesty and if you look upon me with your royal favor, send me to Judah to rebuild the city of my fathers!" (Nehemiah 1:1–11; 2:1–4).

Then I added this to my request: "If it please the king, give me letters to the governors west of the Euphrates River instructing them to let me travel through their countries on my way to Judah; also a letter to Asaph, the manager of the king's forest, instructing him to give me timber for the beams and for the gates of the fortress near the Temple, and for the city walls, and for a house for myself." And the king granted these requests, for God was being gracious to me. (Nehemiah 2:7–8)

Three days after my arrival at Jerusalem I stole out during the night, taking only a few men with me; for I hadn't told a soul about the plans for Jerusalem which God had put into my heart. (Nehemiah 2:11–12)

Take Time to Reflect

1. Note at least five characteristics of Nehemiah's God-Confidence:

2. Write out a prayer expressing your desire to grow in God-Confidence.

3. What key lesson did you glean from today's study?

Confidence Boosters:

- God decides who gets promoted and who doesn't.
- The heart of the king is in the Lord's hands.

Day Three

While You're Waiting for God to Do What He Is Able to Do

You may recall that back in week 4, we gleaned five principles from the Life of Nehemiah. Now we'll discover five more:

1. The Prayer of a God-confident person is rooted in God's Word, consistent with God's character, and based on his promises. Its only objective is the glory of God. Nehemiah's prayer begins with God's character—"O great and awesome God who keeps his promises and is so loving and kind to those who love and obey him!"—and ends by claiming a specific promise: "Oh, please remember what you told Moses . . . 'if you return to me and obey my laws, even though you are exiled to the farthest corners of the universe, I will bring you back to Jerusalem.'"

2. The God-confident person prays, then watches and waits for an opportunity to arise, based on his/her request. Notice that it was "four months later" when Nehemiah got his opportunity to speak to the king. You can be certain he was watching for it all along. When we pray, we should expect God to respond, and live in the light of that expectation, knowing that God's timing may not be the same as ours, but it's always the *right* time.

3. The God-confident person prays before speaking. "With a quick prayer to the God of heaven, I replied." Can you imagine how different our lives would be if, before speaking, we prayed for wisdom, for grace, for God to touch the heart of the hearer?

4. The God-confident person acknowledges every turn of events—and every turn of the human heart—as having been orchestrated by the hand of God. "And the king granted these requests, for God was being gracious to me." Were his requests granted because the king was being gracious? Because he caught the king on a good day, in a cheerful mood? No, they were granted because God was being gracious.

In the book of Ezra, we find another example in which God turned the heart of a king: "because the Lord had filled them with joy by changing the attitude of the king of Assyria, so that he assisted them in the work on the house of God, the God of Israel" (Ezra 6:22 NIV).

If God can turn the heart of a pagan king or a modern-day boss, don't you think he can turn the heart of your husband? Or your mother-in-law? Or your child? Or your pastor? Or anyone else for that matter?

God is God. Changing hearts is what he does for a living. If you're frustrated with someone in your life—especially if it's someone who is in authority over you—call out to the changer-of-hearts. Pray with God-Confidence. Then watch and wait for God to give you the opportunity to make your request known.

5. God-Confidence is quiet confidence. It isn't boastful, because it isn't pursuing its own agenda, but instead seeks God's will. Nehemiah admits, "I hadn't told a soul about the plans for Jerusalem that God had put into my heart" (Nehemiah 2:11 NIV). God-Confidence isn't cocky. It doesn't go around announcing the great things it's going to do for God. Instead, it treasures in its heart the plans God has placed there.

Take Time to Reflect

1. Are your prayers rooted in God's Word, consistent with his character, and derived from his promises? If not, what are your prayers based on?

2. When you pray, do you wait and watch expectantly, confident that God will answer? Or do you promptly forget your prayers? Or perhaps you pray, then rush out, taking matters into your own hands?

3. Do you pray before speaking? How would the words you speak be different if you did?

4. Do you acknowledge every turn of events—and every turn of the human heart—as coming from God?

5. If you want to see a change in your life, write out a prayer asking God to turn the heart of the key person involved in bringing about that change.

6. Do you have quiet confidence? When God places a plan in your heart, can you treasure it there . . . or are you like me: ya gotta blab it?!?

7. What key lesson did you glean from today's study?

Confidence Boosters:

- The God-confident prayer is rooted in God's Word and consistent with God's character.
- God-Confidence acknowledges every turn of events—and every turn of the human heart—as being orchestrated by God.

Day Four

A Civil War Lesson

The Lord is my light and my salvation; he protects me from danger—whom shall I fear? When evil men come to destroy me, they will stumble and fall! Yes, though a mighty army marches against me, my heart shall know no fear! I am confident that God will save me. The one thing I want from God, the thing I seek most of all, is the privilege of meditating in his Temple, living in his presence every day of my life, delighting in his incomparable perfections and glory. Psalm 27:1–4

In describing the woman of virtue, Proverbs 31 says, "She can laugh at the days to come." That's the very essence of God-Confidence: the ability to say, "I don't know what the future holds, but I know who holds the future."

As the Civil War was drawing to a close, the Southern Army would go from town to town, warning the residents to make way for the advancing Northern Army. One day they happened upon a small Virginia farmhouse. They informed the residents that they would have to vacate the premises.

However, the woman responded, "I am a widow, with small children. I have nowhere else to go. This is our home. This is where we'll stay. God has promised to protect us."

Can you imagine the soldiers' response? "Lady, you don't get it. There is an ARMY coming against you. We can't protect you; we can't even protect ourselves."

She insisted. "God will protect us."

The soldiers had other families to notify, so they walked away, shaking their heads. That night the Northern Army did, indeed, pass through, burning and pillaging everything in their path. The next morning, in the midst of the rubble and the ashes, one house stood. It was the house of that widow.

The Southern soldiers returned later to inquire, "Who were those men guarding your house all last night?"

Well, we know who those men were! Psalm 27:1, 3 says, "The Lord is the stronghold of my life—of whom shall I be afraid? Though an army besiege me, my heart will not fear; though war break out against me, even then will I be *confident*" (emphasis added).

Do you have that kind of Total God-Confidence? If an army were coming against you, yet God told you to stand firm, could you do it? More to the point, *how could you do it?* What's the basis of our confidence in the face of overwhelming odds? The character of God. Since our God is *able* to deliver us and *faithful* to keep his promises, we have nothing to fear.

That doesn't mean crummy stuff never happens to Christians. Sometimes God lets the house burn down. My guess is that widow wasn't the only Christian in that small Virginia town. Her house stood. The others fell. But in every case, the purposes of God stood.

Yes, we must have faith in God. We must believe that he is able to deliver us. But we must also trust; trust that if God doesn't deliver us, it's not because he couldn't. It's because he chose not to, for reasons we may—or may not—ever understand.

In order to walk in Total God-Confidence, at some point, faith and trust must merge.

I learned about the merging of faith and trust from another widow. Some months ago, I received an e-mail from one of my readers. She had been blessed by one of my books and wanted to thank me personally. We began a "virtual friendship" and it wasn't long before Kim mentioned that she was heading out to Arizona. She had a story she wanted to tell me. Would I be willing to meet with her? Although I wouldn't advise you to arrange a personal meeting with a cyberfriend, I took the risk. I'm glad I did.

Several weeks ago, Kim Driver and her two daughters, Kristine and Kate, paid us a visit. As the evening progressed, her story unfolded. Kim's husband, Mike, had been a minister in the Assemblies of God for many years, but his heart was always in missions. Throughout their thirteen-year marriage, Kim and Mike visited various parts of the world on short-term mission assignments. Finally, in July 1996, they left for a two-year term in Lithuania. Within three weeks Mike was diagnosed with a brain tumor. Their missionary adventure came to an abrupt end; they returned to the United States. Thousands of people around the world were praying for Mike's recovery. They had faith. Kim had faith. Mike had faith. Within ten weeks Mike was gone.

Was God able? Yes. Was God faithful? Ask Kim. She sees a greater purpose in Mike's death. She and her daughters travel around the country, speaking of God's faithfulness and challenging others with the simple message: "At some point, faith and trust must merge." The God who is able to say yes must be able to say no to his children without their falling apart.

After writing the above paragraphs, it occurred to me that I may have saved Kim's original e-mail. I just checked. I did. Here's a portion of it:

> Since my husband passed away, God has opened doors for me to share the story and my testimony of God's goodness and faithfulness. He has been so good to us, and the things I learned about Him and about myself, even before Mike died, I believe are worth telling. So I have a busy summer full of speaking engagements, and relish the thought of being able to make a difference in someone's life. You know, in a situation like mine, you have to really look for the place where faith and trust collide. I found it, and recently the Lord led me to a portion of Scripture in Daniel 3, verse 17. "The God we serve is ABLE to deliver us. . . . but even if he doesn't . . ." That's the place I had to come to in dealing with Mike's illness. Believing God COULD heal him (that's FAITH), without the guarantee that He would (that's TRUST). Interesting concept, don't you think?

I was blown away that she had quoted the *exact* verse we studied earlier this week. Incredible.

Having met the Driver family, I can tell you that their house is standing amid the rubble and ashes . . . just as surely as the house of that Civil War widow had stood. Have faith and trust collided in your life? If so, your house will surely stand, even if it burns to the ground.[1]

---

[1]You can contact Kim at Trusting Heart Ministries, P.O. Box 9672, Springfield, MO 65801–9672; e-mail: R2girls@aol.com

Take Time to Reflect

1. Recall a miracle in your life; a time when God said yes.

2. Recall a time when God said no. How did you respond?

3. Is the God who is able, able to say no to you without your falling apart?

4. What key lesson did you glean from today's study?

Confidence Boosters:

- If we want to walk in Total God-Confidence, faith and trust must merge.
- The God who is able must be able to say no without our falling apart.

Day Five

Faithful to All Generations

After yesterday's lesson, some of you may have thought, *I don't know if an army is besieging me, but my house certainly looks like it has been under siege*. I want to give a special word of encouragement to moms. At the risk of getting myself into deep trouble, I'd like to especially address stay-at-home moms. Now, you all know I haven't said a word about this subject, so I would be grateful if you single ladies, empty-nesters, working women (and women in other miscellaneous categories I may have overlooked) would indulge me for just one day.

Back to the moms: maybe you've been reading all this stuff about walking in Total God-Confidence, receiving assignments from God, etc., and thinking, *Gee, God's not calling me to be a missionary to Africa. I'm just a mom. I haven't been invited to speak at any women's retreats lately. I don't even have the strength to teach Sunday school. It takes everything I've got just to make it to women's Bible study*.

Do you want to know how I heard about that woman who lived during the Civil War? I'm a personal friend of her great-great-great-great-great-granddaughter, Joy Morse. The true story of her incredible faith has been passed down through the family for nearly one hundred and fifty years. Today the ninth generation of her descendants are walking with the Lord.

If you are searching for significance, search no further. If you are looking for a tough assignment from God, you have one: raising godly kids in this wicked and depraved generation. Put your boots on and get moving!

Yet the question remains: how do we stay motivated to do the small stuff of which motherhood consists? By keeping the big picture in view. By getting a vision for what we can accomplish, not only here and now, but for generations to come and for eternity.

Do you remember the TV series *Dynasty?* That's what I want. Not diamond rings, fabulous clothes, and great hair. (Although I wouldn't mind that great hair.) I want to build a dynasty. A godly dynasty! Ten generations from now, I want my grandchildren talking about the incredible faith of ol' Grandma Donna.

Psalm 127:3 says, "Sons are a heritage from the Lord, children a reward from him." If our children don't *feel* like a reward; if they feel more like a punishment, something's wrong. Our heart is not right. Because God says they are a reward, and his Word is true.

A heritage is something you pass on; something that lives on after you. Children are our opportunity to impact the future. When we are dead and gone. When all our possessions are broken, obsolete, sold at yard sales, or thrown away. When the memories of our accomplishments have long been forgotten and our trophies are collecting dust in the attic, what will remain? When the money and houses and property we leave as an inheritance to our children are spent, worn out, or worthless, what remains?

If we live our lives the way God is calling us to, our godly heritage will remain. I'm not talking about religious tradition. I'm not talking about a denomination. I'm talking about a heritage of a vibrant, living faith passed from generation to generation.

Psalm 78 says,

> *Give ear, O my people, to my law: incline your ears to the words of my mouth. I will open my mouth in a parable: I will utter dark sayings of old: which we have heard and known, and our fathers have told us. We will not hide them from their children, showing to the generation to come the praises of the Lord, and his strength, and his wonderful works that he hath done. For he established a testimony in Jacob, and appointed a law in Israel, which he commanded our fathers, that they should make them known to their children. That the generation to come might know them, even the children which should be born; who should arise and declare them to their children. That they might set their hope in God, and not forget the works of God, but keep his commandments.* (vv. 1–7 KJV)

These verses talk about five generations remaining faithful to God. Our goal as we parent each day should be to pass our faith not only to our children but to our grandchildren.

In the late 1700s, an English woman named Susanna Wesley raised eleven children. She spent thirty minutes of one-on-one time with each of them, every week. She taught them to read the Bible, beginning in Genesis. When she needed time alone with God, she simply pulled her apron over her head. Two of her sons, Charles and John Wesley, were key leaders in the great spiritual awakening of the eighteenth century. We still sing hymns today that they wrote: "O for a Thousand Tongues to Sing," "Hark! the Herald Angels Sing," and many more.[1]

Many historians believe that the Great Awakening was the primary reason England was spared a bloody revolution like the one that occurred in France. Susanna Wesley's children literally changed the course of a nation and impacted the eternal destiny of countless thousands.

Among the men John Wesley led to the Lord was John Taylor. John Taylor heard John Wesley preach on the morning he was to be married and was so moved by what he heard that he ended up late for his own wedding. He was in his barn praying that God would bless his home. John Taylor became a lay Methodist preacher. He was zealous for the Lord and raised up several sons who also became lay Methodist preachers. Those sons had several sons who became . . . you guessed it: lay Methodist preachers.

One of those men had a little boy, who used to listen to his daddy pray every day: "O Lord, please send missionaries to China." When that little boy was six years old, he said, "God, I will go to China." His name was Hudson Taylor. Sound familiar? J. Hudson Taylor grew up to become the founder of the China Inland Mission and the father of the modern faith mission movement.

Ruth Tucker, in her history of Christian missions, writes,

> No other missionary in the nineteen centuries since the apostle Paul has had a wider vision and has carried out a more systematic plan of evangelism across a broader geographic area than Hudson Taylor. In his lifetime, the missionary force under him totaled more than eight hundred and continued to grow in the decades after he died.[2]

---

[1] Kathy McReynolds, *Susanna Wesley* (Minneapolis: Bethany House Publishers, 1998).
[2] Ruth A. Tucker, *From Jerusalem to Irian Jaya* (Grand Rapids, Mich.: Zondervan Publishing House, 1983).

As of this writing, there are nine generations of preachers in the Taylor family—and one of those men is right now a missionary to Thailand. That's a godly dynasty. And it all started where? Susanna Wesley: one woman who had a vision that mothering could make a difference for eternity. One woman with an apron over her head!

Another man impacted by Susanna Wesley's children was Jonathan Edwards, a minister and evangelist who lived in the United States one hundred and fifty years ago. He and his wife had ten children. They passed on to those children a godly heritage. The state of New York did a study on five generations of the Edwards family and found that of their 729 descendants, 300 were preachers, 65 became college professors, 13 were university presidents, 60 were authors, 3 were congressman, and 1 became vice-president of the United States. All from one family who determined to raise godly children; one family who built a godly dynasty.

I want my great-great-great-great-great-great-grandchildren to say, "Thank God, Grandma Donna finally got her priorities straight and slowed down. Thank God, she decided to invest time attending to the 'small stuff' that adds up over time. Thank God, she poured her energy, creativity, and ambition into the lives of her children and, as a result, changed the course of her family history."

I didn't inherit a godly dynasty. But I'm building one for my kids. No matter where you came from, it can start with you.

I know one thing many women struggle with in the midst of all the "small stuff." It is feeling insignificant. Let me ask you this: Would you feel significant if you knew you had the potential to bring 2,187 people to Christ through the impact of your lifetime? Do you know that any woman reading this has the potential to do it? Here's how it works: First, you have three kids and raise them to love the Lord. Then each of those children has three children, and so on. In just seven generations, you'll have led 2,187 people to the Lord. Cool, huh?

I've even got mathematical proof:

$$1 \times 3 = 3$$
$$3 \times 3 = 9$$
$$9 \times 3 = 27$$
$$27 \times 3 = 81$$
$$81 \times 3 = 243$$

$$243 \times 3 = 729$$
$$729 \times 3 = 2,187$$

What could be more exciting than this? If we would only set our hearts upon building a godly dynasty, then we would truly have undertaken the most important job in the world. Not just in rhetoric but in reality.

I recently attended a homeschooling conference featuring Sono Harris, who shared the following excerpt from a book called *The Royal Pathway*:[3]

They will not trouble you long,
children grow up fast.
Nothing on earth grows so fast as children.
It was but yesterday that lad was playing with toys.
He's a man now and gone.
There's no childhood left for him
or for us.
Life has claimed him.
The house has not a child in it.
There's no more noise in the hall,
boys rushing in pell-mell.
There are no more skates or sleds,
bats, balls, or strings left scattered about.
Things are neat enough now.
There is no longer another task before you lie down
of looking after anybody or tucking up the bed clothes.
There are no more disputes to settle,
nobody to get off to practice.
No more fingers to bandage,
no more faces to be washed.
No more rips to mend or shirts to be tucked in.
There never was such peace in the house.
It would sound like music
to have some feet to clatter down the front stairs.
Oh for some children's noise.
What used to ail us that we were

---

[3]The seminar, including the reading of this poem, is available on the audiocassette *Martha vs. Mary* by Sono Harris, Noble Publishing, 1997.

always hushing their loud laughs
and checking their noisy frolic?
Reproving their slamming and banging of doors.
We only wish our neighbors would loan us
an urchin or two to make a little noise
on the premises.
A home without children—
it's like a garden with no flowers,
a lantern with no candle,
a vine with no grapes.
We want to be tired,
to be vexed,
to be run over,
to hear children at work and at play
with all its varieties.
Children are a gift from the Lord,
and they will give us joy if we will let them.

Someday, very soon, life will claim our children. We are only together for a season. Our children will grow up and then the house
will become quiet. Since our time with them is brief, let's make the
most of the summer of child-rearing. Then we can dance into a winter of rich reward rather than shuffling into a season of regret.

In today's culture, it requires Total God-Confidence to keep your
children a priority. May God give you the vision and courage to do it.

Take Time to Reflect

1. What efforts are you making to build a godly dynasty?

2. What more do you need to do?

3. If you continue living as you are now, do you think you'll dance into a winter of rich reward or shuffle into a season of regret?

4. Look up Joshua 1:9 and note God's word of encouragement.

5. Write out a prayer for your children.

6. What key lesson did you glean from today's study?

7. Write out This Week's Verse from memory.

Confidence Boosters:

- Nothing we undertake will have more eternal significance than building a godly dynasty.
- We are only with our children for a season. Then we'll either dance into a winter of rich reward or shuffle into a season of regret.

Weekly Review:

See if you can fill in the ten characteristics of walking in Total God-Confidence. Look in the back of the book if you need help.

C _____ according to his purpose

O _____ to his plan

N _____ by his love

F _____ from the chains that bind

I _____ conformed to his character

D _____ in his word

E _____ by faith

N _____ shaken by the jerks

C _____ that he is able and faithful

E _____ to take the leap of faith

WEEK TEN:
Eager to Take the Leap of Faith

This Week's Verse:

O God, my heart is quiet and confident. No wonder
I can sing your praises!

Psalm 57:7

Day One

Leaping Out of the Nest

*He spreads his wings over them, even as an eagle overspreads
her young. She carries them upon her wings—as does the Lord his
people!*   Deuteronomy 32:11

Christians just love the word picture of soaring eagles. Sounds
good, doesn't it? Our kids are running amok underfoot, but we're just
soaring up above it all. Untouched, undisturbed by the madness of
this world. Nice picture. Too bad it has nothing to do with reality.
Here's what it takes to come to the place where you can mount up
on wings as an eagle:

When the mother eagle is expecting her young, she prepares a
large nest, high on the edge of a cliff. She fashions it out of giant
branches and sharp thorns. Then she fills it with layer upon layer of
soft feathers.

Then, when the baby eagles arrive and start getting all comfy-cozy
in the nest (thinking, *I'm gonna stay here until I'm forty years old*), do
you know what the mother eagle does? She begins to make the nest
increasingly uncomfortable. Each day she removes a few more feathers. Until, finally, the nest becomes unbearable. She does this deliberately, knowing full well that unless she forces her little ones out of
their comfort zone, they'll never take that leap of faith. And if they
never take the leap of faith, they'll never know what it means to *soar*.
That would be tragic indeed, because soaring, after all, is what eagles
were created to do.

Well, finally the little eagles can take it no longer. They climb to
the edge of the nest and look down into the giant chasm below. Their
hearts are gripped with fear, but what they've got is so bad, the un-
known could hardly be worse. They mount their courage and take

the leap of faith, realizing that their wings are completely untested. They have no skill, no experience, no backup plan. They have absolutely no cause for confidence.

The baby eagle continues plummeting toward the earth, and just when it seems all hope is lost, the mother eagle swoops underneath him and allows him to mount up on her wings. For the first time in his life, he *knows* what it means to soar. From that moment on, there's no holding him back. He's free from fear. Confident.

Isaiah 40:31 says, "Those who hope in the Lord will renew their strength. They will soar on wings likes eagles" (NIV).

You know, the only way you'll ever come to that place of "mounting up on wings like eagles" is to take a giant leap of faith. Maybe God has been making you increasingly uncomfortable lately. Maybe he is removing everything that you place your confidence in; deliberately pushing you out of your comfort zone. Maybe he is taking you to a place where all you have left to depend upon is him.

And I've noticed that sometimes he really lets us sweat it. He doesn't swoop under us until the last minute. That's when God-Confidence comes in. That's when we look deep within ourselves and ask, *Is God really able to do what he says? Is he God enough? And is he really FAITHFUL to do what he has promised?*

It boils down to a crisis of confidence. If we really believe God is who he says he is and that he will do what he says he will do, the rest is easy. Okay, so it's not exactly *easy*, but it's definitely easier than the alternative.

When you place your confidence in anyone or anything other than God, do you know what happens? God is compelled to take that source of confidence from you. He won't play second fiddle in your life. Do you want to know what God keeps taking from me? Friends. First, my two best friends moved to Maryland and Massachusetts. Then it got even worse. Would you believe, I've actually had friends move to Malaysia, Mongolia, Morocco, and Mexico?

If by chance, you've been reading this book thinking, *Poor Donna, she doesn't have to stay the kid no one will play with forever. I'll be her friend.* Forget it. The minute you form a friendship with me, the wheels of heaven will be in motion to relocate you to a foreign country beginning with the letter M. And just for the record, MAUI is not a foreign country!

What does God keep taking from you? Is it possible that's the very thing he wants to prevent you from placing your confidence in? God loves you too much to let you put your trust in anyone or anything other than him. That's because he alone is worthy of your confidence.

I can tell you all day long that God is worthy of your confidence. I can tell you that when I was in free-fall, when I had lost *everything* that mattered to me, when I had absolutely nothing left to base my confidence in . . . that was the very moment God swept underneath me and allowed me to soar in a way I never knew possible.

I can tell you this, but until you've let go of everything else; until you've taken that giant leap of faith and found yourself rushing head-long toward apparent destruction; until you're bungee-jumping without a cord; you'll never know—*never really know*—what it's like to have God swoop under you and rescue you; to discover what it means to soar.

I'll tell you that when you've come to that place, faced it and lived to tell about it, all your fear will be gone. You *know* that you *know* that God is there. That he is real. That he is able and faithful. That kind of Total God-Confidence can only come when you, personally, have taken the leap and met God in free-fall. No one can take that leap for you.

And you can't take that leap for anyone else. Not for your husband. Not even for your kids.

It's one thing to take the leap. It's another to watch someone you love taking it. It's almost more than we can bear. That's why we want to meddle and run rescue missions. That's why we want to put some pillows in the nest or offer them the room upstairs. That's why we want to lend them a parachute or rent a helicopter.

It won't work. Until they've taken the leap for themselves and found God faithful, they'll continue thinking they need a rescuer. What they really need is a Savior.

Take the leap. And when it comes time for someone you love to take it, just close your eyes!

Take Time to Reflect

1. Have you ever taken a giant leap of faith? What happened?

2. Is God calling you to take a leap of faith right now? How so?

3. What does God keep taking from you? Could it be the very thing he wants to prevent you from placing your confidence in?

4. Look up Isaiah 55:8–11 and note God's word of encouragement.

5. Write out a prayer asking courage to take your leap of faith.

6. What key lesson did you glean from today's study?

7. Turn to the back of the book and remove your Bible verse card for this week.

Confidence Boosters:

- If we want to soar upon wings as an eagle, we've got to take a giant leap of faith.
- No one can take the leap of faith for us, and we can't take it for anyone else.
- Until you've taken the leap of faith, you'll never truly know that God is there.

Day Two

You Have Not Because You Ask Not

You do not have, because you do not ask.   James 4:2 NRSV

I think the walk of faith requires leaps of faith—and leaps of faith never appear rational to onlookers. We've come to place far too high a premium on human opinion. If we want to soar by faith, then once in a while we've got to take faith-sized risks.

I'm not talking about presumption; you know me better than that by now. I'm talking about faith—the kind of faith that goes out on a limb and risks looking ridiculous. When's the last time you made an absolute fool of yourself *because of your faith*? When's the last time you were surrounded by people scratching their heads, wondering, *What on earth is she thinking?*

Most Christians would be proud to say, "I never look foolish because of my faith. I want everyone to know how rational Christians are, that our faith is rooted in logic. After all, we don't want people thinking Christianity is for extremists and eccentrics."

While there's nothing inherently noble about being an extremist, I worry about Christians who blend into the culture like chameleons. As Josh Harris said, "This country will not survive another generation of Christians that fit in."[1] I worry about Christians who never take any action until they have *all the answers up front*, until they have their safety net in place. I worry about Christians who never do anything that might raise eyebrows.

Granted, you don't want to become irrational in everything you do. So, how do you decide when to conform, when to cling to terra firma, and when to take the leap? I'd like to suggest a very simplistic

---

[1]Josh Harris, *A New Attitude Audio Experience* (Tucker, Ga.: Noble Publishing, 1997).

answer: ask God. And when you ask, ask boldly and specifically, *expecting a specific answer*.

Questions like "God, do you want me to be a better Christian?" don't count. That's a chicken question, since there's no risk of making yourself look ridiculous by acting on the answer! Think of a specific question—one concerning an issue that's puzzling you—then, *ask God* to tell you the answer.

You might be thinking, *Gee, if God has an answer, why on earth didn't he tell me long ago?* But the Bible says, "You do not have, because you do not ask" (James 4:2 NRSV). The immediate context of the verse is referring to material possessions, i.e., you don't have certain *things* because you don't ask (and when you do ask, you ask with wrong motives). But the larger context most certainly refers to wisdom, to answers for life's questions: "If any of you lacks wisdom, he should *ask God* who gives generously to all without finding fault" (James 1:5 NIV [emphasis added]). As Andrew Murray observed, "God's giving is inseparably connected with our asking."[2]

My friend Kim Crabill is the founder of a wonderful ministry called Roses and Rainbows. In 1997 she *asked God* what theme she should choose for their annual women's conference. She asked expecting an answer. As she prayed, she sensed God saying, "Diamonds in the Dust." She asked him to confirm his answer.

A week later she was vacuuming the house, when suddenly she heard the infamous *clank, clank, clank* sound. Her vacuum had swallowed *something* it shouldn't have . . . but what? She opened up the vacuum cleaner bag and there, in the midst of the dust, she found *a diamond* (the stone had fallen out of her wedding ring, without her even noticing). So, do you think God was trying to tell her something, or what?

Hey, wait a minute! Did you just raise your eyebrows? Are you wondering about Kim? Every time Kim tells this story, I'll bet there's at least one listener who thinks she's ridiculous. I LOVE IT!

Why not go do something—or tell a story—that at least *someone* will find absolutely ridiculous. Just be sure you *ask God* first!

---

[2]Leonard Ravenhill, *God's Little Instruction Book on Prayer* (Tulsa: Honor Books, 1996), 59.

Take Time to Reflect

1. When's the last time you raised your eyebrows at something someone did or said?

2. Look up John 10:27–30 and note God's word of encouragement.

3. What do you want to ask God right now? Write out a prayer posing the question below, then watch for the answer.

4. What key lesson did you glean from today's study?

Confidence Boosters:

- Leaps of faith never appear rational to onlookers.
- Ask God—boldly, expecting a specific answer.

Day Three

Your Life Before God

As I looked out the window toward the English Bay, with the city of Vancouver in the distance, my heart ached within me. It had been a tough week, feeling trapped indoors because of the constant rain, unable to understand most of the conversation between my husband and his parents (they speak Farci). I desperately wanted to go to church. Normally when I stay with my in-laws, who are devout Muslims, I have my own private Sabbath celebration. After all the years, I was beyond trying to "win them for Christ" by offending their religious convictions.

This wasn't about flaunting my faith or creating conflict. I knew I needed to be in church. I prayed about it, searched the Yellow Pages for a church, then cautiously approached my husband with my request.

His supportive response was all the confirmation I needed. I quickly dressed, then quietly slipped out the door, headed for church.

The dreary morning matched my mood. It wasn't just about feeling rejected and isolated amid my husband's family. It went deeper. I felt rejected and isolated in general. I don't recall the specifics anymore, but I know it was a time in my life when, no matter how hard I tried to serve God, nothing turned out right. I felt so misunderstood.

I sat alone in the pew of the Christian and Missionary Alliance Church. Scanning through the bulletin, I noticed that they had a guest speaker: a man who had served as a missionary in Vietnam. In my heart, I immediately knew he had something to say that I needed to hear.

He did.

I have tears streaming down my face as I write these words. I just flipped through my Bible, looking for the notations I made that morning. I'll share them with you in a moment, but first, let's look at the passage, 1 Corinthians 4:2–5:

> *Now it is required that those who have been given a trust must*
> *prove faithful. I care very little if I am judged by you or by any*
> *human court; indeed, I do not even judge myself. My conscience*
> *is clear, but that does not make me innocent. It is the Lord who*
> *judges me. Therefore judge nothing before the appointed time; wait*
> *till the Lord comes. He will bring to light what is hidden in dark-*
> *ness and will expose the motives of men's hearts. At that time each*
> *will receive his praise from God.* (NIV)

After reading those words, the missionary shared his story, which I will recount to the best of my recollection. How I wish I'd written down his name or more of the details he shared. (If you're out there, just know that you touched my heart so deeply that I have never been the same.) He went as a missionary to Vietnam, hoping, we can be sure, to serve and glorify God. He worked among the South Vietnamese, preaching the gospel and establishing a church.

Then it happened. The Vietcong attacked the village, pillaging and murdering, with their most vicious actions directed against the church and the believers. As events unfolded, it became clear that the village had been targeted *because of* the missionary's presence. He was, in a very real sense, to blame.

He said he could bear the deaths of the Christians, knowing they would spend eternity in heaven, but what of the nonbelievers? Were they doomed to spend eternity in hell? His ministry was destroyed; his soul was in torment. He left Vietnam a defeated man.

Like most of us, he'd always heard a *portion of* verse 5, taken out of context: "He will bring to light what is hidden in darkness and will expose the motives of men's hearts." The verse had always struck fear in his heart. "Oh no. God's going to uncover my secret, selfish motives and I'm going to be in deep trouble!" He had always heard the verse used in judgment, something like "Even though you may look good to other people, even though your deeds may yield success, God knows you really have an evil heart."

However, as he read through his Bible, he realized that is NOT what verse 5 is about at all. In fact, it means the exact opposite. God was so determined that we NOT miss the meaning, that I believe the

Holy Spirit deliberately guided those who divided the Bible into verses. Notice that verse 5 encompasses three complete sentences, which is rather unusual:

> *Therefore judge nothing before the appointed time; wait till the Lord comes. He will bring to light what is hidden in darkness and will expose the motives of men's hearts. At that time each will receive his* praise *from God* (emphasis added).

This verse isn't speaking of judgment. It's not about bad motives; it's about *good motives.* Yes, God looks at those, too. I just about leaped out of the pew! I was so overjoyed. Here's what I wrote in my Bible:

> He sees our good intentions! He knows how hard I try and how far I've come. He knows how much I love him and *want* to serve him.

I don't know if this happens to you, but so often I *mean well, but perform poorly.* I have the greatest of intentions, but no matter how hard I try, everything turns out all wrong. In those moments, I cling to this verse. I turn away from those who criticize me and look to the Father: "Lord, you know my heart. I know I've made another huge mess, but I meant well. Father, judge me according to my motives, not according to my success."

I also included a notation on verse 3, where Paul writes, "I care very little if I am judged by you." I underlined "very little" and added: "Not a lot—we should give it consideration; but don't overestimate it." That is, if almost everyone is giving you the thumbs down, you should seriously consider whether or not there's some merit to their criticism. But don't let their opinions overwhelm and incapacitate you.

Live your life before God . . . and God alone. People may misunderstand you, misjudge you. They may reject you or mock you. None of that matters. Live your life before God. Let him be your judge. Then when you stand before him, be ready to receive not judgment, but praise.

Take Time to Reflect

1. Have you previously thought this passage was talking about "bad motives"? If so, describe the freedom that comes from knowing God sees your "good motives" and will praise you, even when people judge you.

2. Can you think of an occasion when you "meant well" but things turned out badly? Bring it before God, asking him to judge your heart, not your results.

3. Look up 1 Peter 5:6–11 and note God's word of encouragement for you.

4. What key lesson did you glean from today's study?

Confidence Boosters:

- God sees our *good intentions*.
- Live your life before God alone.

Day Four

Another Bird Story

Since we started this week with a bird story, I have birds on my mind. I'd like to share another one of my bird stories with you. And for those of you who still have any doubts about just how eccentric I really am, this will put those doubts to rest.

I was walking through a park one day, when I noticed a tiny little bird trying to keep pace with me. I found this amusing . . . it doesn't take much. So I quickened my step; he quickened his; his tiny legs were going 100 miles per hour. "Aha, so you want to race," I declared aloud, and started walking even faster. The poor little creature was out of breath by now and I thought to myself, "You silly bird, how can you possibly win? Can't you see that my legs are about one thousand times the length of yours?"

Just then, the bird took flight . . . and landed about twenty yards ahead of me.

So which one of us really has the bird brain?

Anyway, it just goes to show that appearances are often deceiving. If someone had been watching our race—someone who didn't understand the true nature of the bird—he would have thought that bird didn't have a chance. He would have concluded that the obstacle was insurmountable.

It's the same with us. The obstacles in our lives may seem insurmountable. People may even look at our lives, and think, "You silly woman. Do you honestly think you have a chance of overcoming?" But you have a secret power they know nothing about. You have the power to soar. No matter what you're up against, just remember: with God's help, you can always take flight and overcome.

I remember a time in my life when the obstacles seemed insurmountable; when God was calling me to do something I thought was impossible. Anyone looking at my life at that point would have concluded that I was utterly defeated.

In the midst of the trial, I remember sitting in church one morning, feeling hopeless. I looked around me, and thought, "No one here understands what I'm going through. They have no idea who I really am. No one here even likes me."

Just then, I felt as if someone had wrapped his arms around me. It was the most all-encompassing hug I had ever experienced. I felt love and warmth flood over me, from my head all the way down to my feet. As my heart began to soar in the beauty of that moment, I realized . . . it was God who hugged me.

Then he spoke these words to my heart: "I like you, Donna. I like you just the way you are." I can't tell you what that meant. Sure, we've all heard "God loves you. He has a wonderful plan for your life." But the idea that God liked me was just incredible!

Talk about taking flight! There wasn't an obstacle on earth I couldn't have surmounted at that moment. I was truly ready to take that leap of faith! Ready to do anything God might call me to, confident of his love and affection for me.

Maybe you have a hard time believing that God likes you; maybe you don't even like yourself. But it's true. God not only loves you; he likes you. I know I've been telling you for ten weeks to *walk* in Total God-Confidence; but now I think I've got a better idea: Take flight and *soar with Total God-Confidence*.

I'll be looking for you in the sky!

Take Time to Reflect

1. Is there an obstacle in your life that seems insurmountable?

2. Write out a prayer expressing your confidence that with God's help you can indeed take flight and overcome.

3. Do you know, truly know in your heart, that God not only loves you, he likes you? If not, ask God to impress that truth upon your heart.

4. What key lesson did you glean from today's study?

Confidence Boosters:

- No matter what the obstacle, with God's help, you can always take flight and overcome it.
- God not only loves you, he likes you.

Day Five

At the End of the Leap

I didn't want to share this story. It's too personal; too painful. But having reread day 1 about the leap of faith, I knew it was cowardly of me to keep silent. Here goes.

In November of 1996 our family was in flat-out crisis mode. For many months we'd been coming under pressure to "get rid of Nikki." There were many people who felt we shouldn't have taken her in to start with. I began to listen to the growing cacophony of voices: Christians and non-Christians. Family and non-family. The consensus was clear: Our efforts to save Nikki were destroying the rest of our family.

Everything came to a head during the visit of my spiritual mentor, whom I'll call Sue. This was the woman I had idolized for seventeen years. If it came from her lips, I figured it was direct from the throne room of God. Time after time, when I was unclear about what direction to take, unclear what God was trying to communicate to me, rather than turning to him, I'd turn to Sue. It was almost as if I'd stick my head out the window and yell, "Have you heard anything from God concerning me?" I had no confidence in my own ability to hear his voice; no confidence in my relationship with him. Instead, I placed my confidence in Sue.

I should have known God would have to knock down that idol. And he did.

Sue spent a week in my home, and concluded, "Donna, it's great that you want to rescue Nikki, but you've abandoned your own children in the process. You've got to get rid of her, and the time to act is right now. You haven't a moment to waste." After countless hours of discussion and endless prayer vigils over the next few days, I was convinced she was right. (I hadn't yet learned the lesson that "God's will is not a crisis.")

I had to concede that life had become difficult; that Leah had paid a heavy emotional price, going from only child to middle child. Leah had also felt the full fury of Nikki's anger and other pent-up emotions. Sometimes Leah was afraid of Nikki. Sometimes. . . . I was afraid of her.

I went into Nikki's room and sat on her bed. I tried to explain that I loved her, but the price had just become too high. She begged me not to do it.

I put her in the car and drove her to a friend's house. I'll never forget the feeling in the pit of my stomach as I watched her walking away; walking into her fifty-first home. I thought my heart would explode.

By now, seemingly everyone in the church and community knew of our turmoil. Everyone had an opinion. I thought my head would explode.

I was in total free-fall. Emotionally. Spiritually. I was enveloped in darkness. I knew that unless God came to my rescue, I was going to crash.

That night I learned what it means to wrestle with God in prayer. I felt that he was asking me to bring Nikki back into my home, but I needed a promise. I needed to know that, if I did, he would take care of my precious Leah and my sweet, innocent baby Tara.

On November 16, 1996, God gave me the promise I'd asked for. I wrote it down:

"If you will be faithful to what I am asking you to do, I will bring you to a place of healing and restoration . . . with goats."

When I awoke early the next morning, the Holy Spirit prompted me to turn to Lamentations 3:19–23:

> I remember my affliction and my wandering, the bitterness and the gall. I well remember them, and my soul is downcast within me. Yet this I call to mind and therefore I have hope: Because of the Lord's great love we are not consumed, for his compassions never fail. They are new every morning; great is your faithfulness. (NIV)

Later that same morning we brought Nikki home. We had yet to see what God's faithfulness would bring about.

As a family, we had long talked and dreamed of moving to a "gentleman's farm," a place where we would have some land to plant a garden and raise animals. We also dreamed of having a guest house where friends, pastors, and missionaries could come to be refreshed. We even talked of having a mini-retreat center so that, rather than flying all over the country, people could fly to us.

From the time I was a little girl, I dreamed of being a writer. I pictured myself nestled in a cabin in the mountains, surrounded by woods and the beauty of God's creation. Lastly, having worked from home since 1989, I dreamed of having my office in a separate building.

One thing we never dared to dream was that all these dreams would come true *in one place*.

A year after I took my famous leap of faith, we began house-hunting. On our third outing, we visited a property with a huge cedar-sided house nestled on two wooded acres, situated on the side of a mountain. The house was rustic on the outside, which made my heart sing. Writers just love rustic. But it was completely modern on the inside—having been built just three years earlier—which made my not-even-slightly-handy husband breathe a sigh of relief.

As a bonus, the property also had a large separate building featuring a 24' x 24' office; a complete guest house with bedroom, bathroom, kitchen, and living room; and an unfinished 24' x 24' room that would be perfect for a prayer chapel/seminar room.

Not only that, unlike most of the other homes we had looked at, the property was zoned for livestock. Yes, we could have goats.

Ready for the clincher? The buyer was motivated, to say the least. They sold us the house for half of what it was worth, and since we couldn't find a buyer for our house, *they bought it*.

Now, that's what I call a God thing!

That's what I call soaring!

Just to bring you up-to-date on our family: we're not perfect, but we're doing great. Leah loves our new country lifestyle. She adores the goats, dogs, and rooster, not to mention all the ladybugs, butterflies, praying mantises, and who knows what else she's managed to find. Tara adores *both* of her big sisters and it does my heart good to think the only life she'll ever know is the life we have here together.

We've put our extra building, which we've dubbed "Restoration House," to excellent use. I'm sitting in the office right now, writing this book! The guest house has been occupied, and hearts have been refreshed. This past weekend, we had our first on-site ladies' retreat with twenty-four women. It was a great success.

Nikki is totally on fire for God and has the gift of evangelism. She speaks at teen conferences around the country, sharing her message called "Finally Home." God has used her as a vessel to bring dozens of teenagers into a relationship with Christ. She's currently writing her first book, *Finally Home*.

After working her fingers to the bone to raise $5,000 (as you may recall, she raised it a dollar at a time), she spent last summer as a missionary in South Africa. Out of some two thousand applicants, she was selected as one of the top–20 finalists for Focus on the Family's 1998 BRIO Girl Competition. One of the judges, BRIO's Beauty and Fashion editor, Andrea Stevens, was so impressed with Nikki's personal interview that she invited Nikki to speak to a group of two hundred teen girls at her church.

Nikki hopes to be a pastor's wife, with a speaking and writing ministry on the side. She is now sixteen years old, has graduated from homeschool high school, and plans to start Bible college in the fall.

Two years have given me some perspective on what our family lived through, although I don't think I'll ever understand everything. I'm now convinced that the forces of hell were trying to drive Nikki from our home. The enemy of her soul knew what God was planning to accomplish through her life, and he came to steal, kill, and destroy. Instead, we were able to mount up on wings as an eagle. And today we're soaring.

It all started with a leap of faith.

Why not take one of your own?

Wow, I just realized something: this is our last day together! I hope these ten weeks have strengthened you for the journey ahead and equipped you to walk each day in Total God-Confidence. Thanks for letting me share my life with you. If it's made a difference, I would love to hear from you. You'll find my address in the front of this book.

I leave you with a benediction:

> *May God himself, the God of peace, sanctify you through and through. May your whole spirit, soul and body be kept blameless*

at the coming of our Lord Jesus Christ. The one who calls you is faithful and he will do it. (1 Thessalonians 5:23–24 NIV)

Take Time to Reflect

1. Have you ever had an experience where the majority opinion was the opposite of what you believed God was calling you to do?

2. How did you handle it and what were the results?

3. Look up John 8:32 and note God's word of encouragement.

4. What key lesson did you glean from today's study?

5. What were the most important lessons you've learned from your ten-week journey to walking in Total God-Confidence?

6. Write out a prayer thanking God for the lessons you have learned.

7. Write out This Week's Verse from memory.

Confidence Boosters:

- You can't soar until you take the leap of faith.
- Sometimes the majority is wrong.

Weekly Review:

See if you can fill in the ten characteristics of walking in Total God-Confidence. Look in the back of the book if you need help.

C _____ according to his purpose

O _____ to his plan

N _____ by his love

F _____ from the chains that bind

I _____ conformed to his character

D _____ in his Word

E _____ by faith

N _____ shaken by the jerks

C _____ that he is able and faithful

E _____ to take the leap of faith

Steps to Freedom

1. Know that God loves you: "For God so loved the world that he gave his one and only Son, that whoever believes in him shall not perish but have eternal life" (John 3:16)*.

2. Acknowledge your sin. "For all have sinned and fall short of the glory of God" (Romans 3:23).

3. Turn from sin. "Therefore do not let sin reign in your mortal body so that you obey its evil desires. Do not offer the parts of your body to sin, as instruments of wickedness, but rather offer yourselves to God" (Romans 6:12–13).

4. Accept that Jesus is the only way. "I am the way and the truth and the life. No one comes to the father except through me" (John 14:6). "Salvation is found in no one else, for there is no other name under heaven given to men by which we must be saved" (Acts 4:12).

5. Realize that Jesus paid the penalty for your sins. "But he was pierced for our transgressions, he was crushed for our iniquities; the punishment that brought us peace was upon him, and by his wounds we are healed. We all, like sheep, have gone astray, each of us has turned to his own way; and the Lord has laid on him the iniquity of us all" (Isaiah 53:5–6).

6. Receive Jesus as Savior. "Here I am! I stand at the door and knock. If anyone hears my voice and opens the door, I will go in and eat with him, and he with me" (Revelation 3:20). "Yet to all who received him, to those who believed in his name, he gave the right to become children of God" (John 1:12).

---

*The Scripture quotations for these steps are taken from the New International Version of the Bible.

A Note to Leaders

Dear Bible study leaders:

I want to thank you for choosing *Walking in Total God-Confidence*, not only for your own use, but to share with the women God has entrusted to your care. It's a great honor to know that, among all the excellent Bible study materials available, you consider my book worthwhile.

It's my fervent prayer that leading this study will be a blessing and not a burden to you. As I pondered whether or not I wanted to write another book—and came up with the answer, "What! am I crazy?"—God assured me that "This time, the burden will be light." He made good on his promise. This book was a joy to write and I hope it will be a joy to teach, as well.

I pray that this journey will lead you into a deeper love relationship with God and into closer fellowship with the women who participate.

When I wrote *Becoming a Vessel God Can Use*, I urged readers to take the study one day at a time; to resist the temptation to rush through. I have since heard—from many people that I don't even know—how to read my own books! The best way, so I'm told, is to quickly read through the entire book, without looking at the questions. You might instruct the women in your group to set aside a day or a long weekend to tackle the project. Then, once they have the overview, they can work through the book, one day at a time.

Another piece of feedback I'd like to pass along is this: Whenever possible, use a visual. When we talk about "putting on the boots," wear boots to class. When we talk about being a PWA (Princess With an Attitude), wear a tiara. Not only that, bring enough materials for each of the ladies to make her own tiara. There's also a lesson about elephants. You obviously can't bring a *real* one, but do bring a stuffed elephant with a rope around its ankle.

Well, you get the idea. Bring the study to life, and it will bring life to the lives of those who participate. Speaking of participants, I'm including a Participant Profile Worksheet. Please make photocopies of it to use with your class. During your first meeting, ask each person to complete the questionnaire. Allow plenty of time for this exercise. The insight you will gain will be extremely valuable as you seek to meet the needs of each woman. Once everyone has finished, spend time discussing their responses *but don't call on anyone.* People do not like to be "put on the spot," so let them know from the beginning that your policy is to encourage—but not require—participation in the discussion.

Make it a point to contact each woman on a regular basis, *outside* the classroom environment. It could be a phone call, a note card, or a trip to the park together. The key is to demonstrate a personal interest in their spiritual growth and well-being. The profile sheets will give you a good place to start in understanding each woman's needs and in initiating conversation.

The one exception to the "no putting people on the spot" rule are the memory verse cards, which you'll find at the back of the book. Each week, at the very beginning of class, ask each woman to recite her verse from memory. Do it in a spirit of fun and out of a desire to "spur one another on toward love and good deeds." Be sensitive, and avoid embarrassing anyone. Nevertheless, when the women come to understand that they will be expected to recite their verse, almost all will rise to the occasion and put in the extra effort required.

If women will carry their memory verse cards with them wherever they go, there is absolutely no reason why they can't memorize one verse per week. You may find it helpful to review the tips provided in week 6, day 4, "Knowing God's Word by Heart." Using these techniques, anyone can learn to memorize Scripture effectively.

Along with each week's memory verse, I have also included a few key thoughts to summarize the lesson. These do not have to be memorized, but will help the women get the most out of the study.

Finally, you'll notice that there is a Weekly Review Test included each week. It's always the same test, but hopefully the women will get better and better scores. Again, make it a point to take the test as a group every week by reciting in unison the ten characteristics of walking in Total God-Confidence.

When your group successfully completes the study, I would love nothing more than to receive a photograph of all you beautiful ladies. I like to put these on the wall of my home office to prevent me from "growing weary in well-doing." I really cherish every letter I receive, although I must admit I'm not that great about writing back. Just know in advance, you'll do the heart of this princess some good!

His vessel,

Donna Partow
P.O. Box 842
Payson, AZ 85541
donnapartow@cybertrails.com

Participant Profile Worksheet

Name: _____   Phone: _____

Address: _____

_____

_____

Reason for enrolling in this class: _____

_____

_____

_____

_____

What is the most pressing problem/challenge in your life right now?

_____

_____

_____

How can this class (and your fellow classmates) help you cope more effectively?

_____

_____

_____

_____

How do you want your life to be different at the end of this study?

_____

_____

_____

_____

What are some specific habits you want to improve on?

_____

_____

_____

_____

_____

List five things you expect from a women's Bible study. (Indicate things you like/dislike.)

1. _____

2. _____

3. _____

4. _____

5. _____

Thinking back on prior experiences with Bible studies, what motivated you to finish a class? What might cause you to drop out?

_____

_____

_____

_____

How can your leader help you get the most out of this class?

_____

_____

_____

_____

_____

The Characteristics of Those Who Walk in Total God-Confidence

- CALLED according to his purpose
- OPEN to his plan
- NOURISHED by his love
- FREE from the chains that bind
- INCREASINGLY conformed to his character
- DAILY in his Word
- ENERGIZED by faith
- NOT shaken by the jerks
- CONVINCED that he is able and faithful
- EAGER to take the leap of faith

Make a Difference in Your World.

A Ten-Week Journey to

Becoming A Vessel GOD CAN USE

Donna Partow

Feel overwhelmed by life's pressures? Find new confidence and significance through this remarkably honest portrait of how God can accomplish extraordinary things through ordinary people.

What does it take to be a woman God can use? Do you have to be perfect? Do your spices have to be in alphabetical order? In *Becoming a Vessel God Can Use*, Donna Partow shows how God can accomplish extraordinary things through ordinary people. This ten-week study for groups or individuals explores both biblical and contemporary examples, including the author's personal journey from drug dealer to Christian communicator.

The key, according to Partow, is recognizing that God is the potter and we are the clay. He is constantly about the business of transforming us into vessels He can use. The sometimes painful process includes being:

- **Emptied of self**—letting go of both our pain from the past and our dreams for the future.
- **Cleansed**—using five tools of spiritual cleansing.
- **Filled**—with the Living Water, not just religious doctrines and rituals.
- **Then poured** into the lives of others, as God directs.

Popular around the world, *Becoming a Vessel God Can Use* is a powerful life-changing journey you don't want to miss!

Available from your nearest Christian bookstore (800) 991-7747 or from Bethany House Publishers.

BETHANY HOUSE PUBLISHERS

11400 Hampshire Ave. South
Minneapolis, MN 55438
www.bethanyhouse.com